# C. S. Lewis
## Life at the Center

*Perry C. Bramlett*

PEAKE ROAD

Macon, Georgia

ISBN 1-57312-054-5

*C. S. Lewis: Life at the Center*

Perry C. Bramlett

Copyright © 1996
Peake Road

6316 Peake Road
Macon, Georgia 31210-3960
1-800-747-3016

Peake Road
is an imprint of
Smyth & Helwys Publishing, Inc.®

*Library of Congress Cataloging-in-Publication*

Bramlett, Perry C.
    C. S. Lewis: life at the center / Perry C. Bramlett.
    viii + 88 pp.        5.5" x 8.5" (14 x 21.5 cm.)
    Includes bibliographical references.
    ISBN 1-57312-054-5 (alk. paper)
    1. Lewis, C. S. (Clive Staples), 1898–1963.
    2. Spiritual life—Christianity—History—20th century.
    I. Title.
    BX5199.L53B73        1996
    283'.092—dc20                        96-14322
    [B]                                        CIP

# Contents

## Appendixes

# Preface

Although C. S. Lewis has been called "the apostle to the skeptics" and "the man who made Christianity intellectually respectable," it is a source of comfort and inspiration to many persons to know that he also had a disciplined prayer life, read his Bible devotionally, and had many close and nurturing friendships. Yet, he was never pretentious and never has been accused of "spiritual arrogance," even by those who disagreed with him on religious or literary matters. It took him a long time to become a believer and follower of Christ; indeed, Lewis was a very reluctant convert. Once he became a committed Christian, however, he never forgot the basics of his faith.

The basics of prayer, devotion to the Scriptures, and friendship helped balance Lewis's Christian life between the intellectual and the pragmatic, between knowing and doing. And in the long process of growing and maturing, C. S. Lewis became a little like Christ, something he mentioned in *Mere Christianity* as the goal for every Christian.

When I speak about Jack (as his friends knew him) Lewis to churches, I am always asked about his prayer life and how he used and approached (read) the Bible. Also, I am asked about his friends and how they influenced him. I often comment that when reading Lewis, one will often sense that "this man was close to God." One reason he is so trusted and read today is that his warm and authentic piety shines through his work.

Despite the great appreciation of and respect for C. S. Lewis, his piety and his works, literature about his spirituality—what I call his "life at the center"—has been lacking. The major studies of his life all have anecdotes about his spirituality, but only a few books and articles—not counting the biographies—have been written containing significant sections about Lewis's prayer life, and most of these are now out of print.

Similarly, little has been written about Lewis and his devotion to the Scriptures. I am fortunate to have in my library well over one hundred books and twelve hundred articles about him or that contain significant sections about him. Not including the nine biographical works, only four of the books have any type of discussion about Lewis and the Bible, however. Twenty or so of the articles are concerned with what he thought about the Bible or how he approached it for reading and study. Only one complete book has been written about C. S. Lewis and the Bible.

As for his friends, most of what has been written about them and their influence on his spiritual life is contained in the biographies. A few other works include reminiscences and insights into Lewis's relationships with close friends such as J. R. R. Tolkien and Charles Williams; his life as a spiritual mentor; and his friendships with colleagues, students, and other admirers. Several collections of Lewis's letters are available; and while these contain valuable details about Jack as a faithful friend, they are often general in nature and do not provide specifics about his spirituality.

Because literature about Lewis and prayer and scripture and friends is limited, I wrote this book for two reasons: (1) to "fill a gap" in C. S. Lewis studies for the general reader and non-Lewis specialist, whether layperson or minister, and (2) to answer questions about his spiritual life. It is my aim to present him as a wonderful example for the Christian who is serious about his or her own spiritual pilgrimage. It is my hope that this book will not only provide information about that "life at the center," but that it also will be an inspiration to those who are seeking such a life. We could scarcely hope to have a better model.

# Acknowledgements

Some of the ideas for this book grew from a series of Lenten lectures on C. S. Lewis that I presented to the St. Luke's Episcopal Church in Birmingham, Alabama, in early 1994. My heartfelt thanks go to the pastor, John R. Claypool, and his staff and church for their many kindnesses and courtesies. I will always believe that my time at St. Luke's was and will remain a high point in my C. S. Lewis teaching ministry to churches.

I owe very special thanks and gratitude to several people, starting with Fred and Elizabeth Lane of Chesapeake, Virginia. Fred and Liz have always been there for me, and I regard them as part of my own family. I know of no other people who exemplify more what it means to be faithful (and longsuffering) Christian friends. My pastor, Ron Higdon, and his wife, Pat, also deserve my thanks, and much more. I look up to both of them as the very best models of Christian friendship.

I am very fortunate to have as friends several people who knew C. S. Lewis personally and have studied him for years. I have been enriched often by their knowledge, encouragement, and advice. Kay Lindskoog of Orange, California, has been my unofficial "C. S. Lewis mentor." Without her encouragement, I might not have started a new ministry nearly six years ago at age forty-four. Kay has taught me much about Lewis, the "Lewis industry," the craft of writing, and the persistence of faith during great duress. Sheldon Vanauken of Lynchburg, Virginia, has been a good friend through letters for several years. As someone who came to the Christian faith largely due to the influence of C. S. Lewis, Van has shared with me a bounty of observations and insights that I could obtain nowhere else. Other friends who have helped me learn more about C. S. Lewis are George Sayer of Malvern, England, and Douglas Gresham of County Carlow, Ireland. To all of these I can only say, "Thank you."

I am grateful also to other friends and colleagues for their support and confidence. Among these are Henlee Barnette, David and Kelly Freeman, Jim and Sissy Grote, Evarose Gutmann, Marc Jolley, Mark Medley, Duane and Debbie Musgrove, Nan O'Neal, and the ladies of the Ruth Sunday School class at Broadway Baptist Church in Louisville, Kentucky. All of these good and very valued friends have helped me much more than they realize.

I would also like to thank the folks at Smyth and Helwys Publishing for their trust in an unknown author, and especially for their willingness to publish a book about C. S. Lewis. They have shown me kindness and foresight that I will not forget.

This book is dedicated to my wife, Joan. Her faith, love, and patience have kept me going through these times of creativity and much change. I can only hope and pray that all authors have such a good and steadfast companion.

# Chapter 1

"Life at the Center"

# The Life of C. S. Lewis

Clive Staples (C. S.) Lewis is recognized as the greatest Christian defender of the faith in the twentieth century. In fact, during his lifetime and since his death, he may have influenced more people for the cause of Jesus Christ and his church than perhaps anyone in this century. He was the most famous Christian in the world from about the middle 1940s until his death in 1963; and he still may be the most famous Christian in the world, if the ever increasing sales of his books and the attention now given to him are any indication.

Born in Belfast, Ireland, to Scotch and Welsh parents, he lived most of his life in the university city of Oxford. He was a big, red-nosed, rumpled, jolly man—he looked like a prosperous, red-nosed farmer.[1] He had a booming laugh, a superb speaking voice, and a large measure of personal magnetism or charisma.

C. S. Lewis was a prolific writer who wrote works of Christian science fiction and theology for the average person. He wrote books about love, hell, temptation, miracles, suffering, grief, prayer, ethics, and the Bible. A frequent theme in almost all of his books is heaven.[2] He wrote about his own conversion and also wrote wonderful books for children. He contributed some of the finest letters ever written. He was an underrated poet and appreciated literary critic and wrote several hundred essays, book reviews, and articles for newspapers, other people's books, and scholarly journals.

C. S. Lewis was one of those extraordinary Christians who had the remarkable gift of being able to change lives. Scores of people from all over the world have testified how he led them to new faith in Christ or how he helped make their old faith "come alive." He is also one of the very few Christian authors who is read extensively by non-Christians.

Lewis was a spiritual pilgrim. Reared in the church, he left it as a teenager and became a practicing atheist. He once wrote to his boyhood and lifelong friend Arthur Greeves, "I believe in no religion. There is no proof for any of them."[3] In many of those days away from the faith, Jack was not a very nice person. Late in his life he wrote this tribute to Greeves:

He was not a clever boy, he was even a dull boy . . . He had no "ideas" . . . I bubbled over with them . . . he had feelings to offer, feelings which more mysteriously—for he was always very inarticulate—he taught me to share . . . I learned charity from him and failed . . . to teach him arrogance in return.[4]

For many years Lewis really was an arrogant intellectual. He became a believer in God with great reluctance, which he wrote about in his autobiography. During World War II, he spoke on the BBC (British Broadcasting Corporation) about his faith and became an overnight sensation. Millions of people listened to this highly educated man who could think in five languages talk about God and "basic" Christian doctrines. The flood of mail that followed these fifteen-minute talks made him famous all over Europe.

A few years later he became even more well-known. While walking out of church one morning, he was struck by an idea for a very unusual book. The book would consist of letters from one devil to another on the art of temptation. The excitement over the publication of *The Screwtape Letters* put Lewis on the cover of *Time* magazine and made him celebrated in the United States.

For the first time in his life, C. S. Lewis had some money. He was financially prosperous for the rest of his life, but gave much of his wealth to charities. He continued teaching, writing, and lecturing at Oxford. In the early 1950s, he wrote seven children's books called *The Chronicles of Narnia*, which have become international bestsellers and have been made into plays and television "events." Also in the 1950s, he maintained his writing and teaching career at Cambridge University.

Lewis once said he lived a "pretty routine life." He surprised the readers of *Time* by stating that he did indeed enjoy monotony.[5] While without a doubt one of the great minds of the twentieth century, in his letters he often wrote about simple things: his illnesses, his pets, the books he was reading, his friends. Jack and his brother lived in the same house, "The Kilns," in the Oxford suburb of Headington for thirty years. He sat in the same pew in his home church, Holy Trinity, for thirty years—a pew that now has a special marker commemorating that fact.

For recreation, Jack and his special friends would take walking tours for up to fifty miles in the glorious English countryside. At home, he and his brother Warren would entertain friends and listen to classical music—Wagner and Beethoven were among their favorites. They would read and drink a cup of tea or glass of port before bedtime, which was usually 10:30 or 11 o'clock. The brothers spent much of their time answering letters.

C. S. Lewis averaged receiving 100 letters a week, beginning in the late 1940s and continuing for the remainder of his life. He answered every one of those letters; he considered it a duty and a ministry. During the week he was a tutor, lecturer, and spiritual mentor. He was in almost constant demand as a preacher and speaker. Lewis and William Temple were the only people in those days who could regularly "fill the pews" every time they preached at Oxford's famed University Church.[6]

Based on what has been written and said about Lewis by those who knew him, several facets of his personality come into sharp focus. For one, the pictures in books and how he is portrayed in films and plays do not do him justice. He was fairly tall, had a very ruddy complexion and dark eyes, and wore the same hat for years (he hated to "shop").[7] His hair was retreating rapidly from his forehead, and you can see that he loved to eat and drink the local brews of Oxford's pubs. What the pictures don't show is his aliveness. His expression was always changing, "lighting up." His friend Christopher Derrick described Lewis as "jovial," "a man who enjoyed the world," "not a man to stand on his dignity," and "merry."[8]

Lewis was not self-conscious and did not act like a celebrity. He lived very modestly. The barmaid at one of his favorite pubs always spoke of him with great respect, but to her he was simply "Mr. Lewis of Magdalen College." The lady was astounded when she found out that he was "famous" and had written many books. When he talked, particularly in the broadcast talks, he often reminded people of his books. He was straight to the point, never at a loss for the exact word.

He had an incredible memory. His pupil Kenneth Tynan recalls playing "memory games" with Lewis. He would pull any volume from Lewis's large library down from the shelf and quote any line from the unnamed book. Lewis could not only give the title, he could quote verbatim the rest of the page![9]

Ronald W. Higdon, pastor of Broadway Baptist Church in Louisville, Kentucky, sometimes uses a beautiful phrase in his sermons that describes very well how Lewis dealt with people. That phrase is "the common courtesy of Jesus Christ." Lewis never patronized or treated people discourteously. Indeed, he had a reputation for charity that went beyond helping people with monetary needs, which he did often. For much of his adult life, after he started making money, Lewis gave at least two-thirds of his book royalties to charities. His friend John Lawlor once called him "one of the most cheerful givers, according to his means, who ever lived."[10]

A story that illustrates Lewis's "common courtesy of Christ" toward everyone he met was told by Jill Flewett Freud, who lived at The Kilns during World War II after her home was destroyed by German bombs. During the war, a mentally handicapped man also lived at The Kilns. Lewis attempted to teach the alphabet to this man during his stay there. Every evening he would make drawings and letter cards and go through the alphabet with the man and try to teach him small words. Jill Freud wrote,

> I don't think he had a great deal of success because the young man found it hard to retain anything. But for more than two months Jack Lewis went through the alphabet with him every evening.[11]

In his day Lewis was the finest lecturer at Oxford. With his deep, resonant voice, the clearness of his presentations, his wit, and his "personality," one can understand why. His lectures, which were not mandatory, were the best attended at Oxford by students. He would stroll into a lecture hall talking, walk up to the front, give his pocket watch to a student, remind the student to remind him of the time, and continue talking. He would often end his lectures by talking on his way out.

He always had close friends. One group of his friends, "the Inklings," has become much celebrated in literary and religious history. The splendid detective story writer Edmund Crispin wrote this line in one of his stories: "There goes C. S. Lewis; it must be Tuesday."[12] This must have been said more than once as Lewis was spotted entering his favorite pub— "The Eagle and Child" (known locally as "The Bird and Baby")—with J. R. R. Tolkien, Charles Williams, and other friends.

For more than twenty years, they would gather there once a week for their favorite stout, and on Thursday evenings they would meet in Lewis's rooms at Magdalen College. The Inklings would talk about philosophy, religion, and politics, and would read aloud from the books they were writing. One friend who attended the Inklings meetings wrote later, "The best of them were as good as anything I shall live to see."[13]

Jack Lewis was a bachelor until the age of fifty-nine. He surprised everyone by marrying a forty-one-year-old New Yorker who was an ex-atheist, an ex-member of the American Communist Party, an ex-Hollywood screenwriter, a divorcée, a novelist and poet, the mother of two small boys, and a Jewish convert to Christianity. He married her twice: the first time in a civil ceremony to keep her from being deported to America (probably for her past communist activities), the second time in a religious ceremony at the hospital where she had been diagnosed terminally ill with bone and breast cancer.

Helen Joy Davidman Gresham and Jack Lewis had an uncommonly good marriage while it lasted—a little more than three years. After her death by the same disease that killed his mother and father and favorite aunt, he wrote about his grief in a little book that has helped thousands.[14] Only three years after his wife's death, Lewis died at his Oxford home.

### The Effectiveness of Lewis

C. S. Lewis's abilities as a writer and his qualities as a Christian have had a profound effect on persons, both Christian and non-Christian. He wrote with great clearness and presented his ideas in a way that most reasonably intelligent people can understand. He was open-minded and ready to dialogue with anyone, whether they agreed with him or not. He found Christianity to be thoroughly creditable and to make sense, and in his writings convinces his readers that he was a reliable guide to faith. He often used everyday situations and stories to make theology and doctrine easier to understand. In addition, Lewis used a great deal of humor to make difficult subjects palatable.

He also possessed to a high degree the great virtue of honesty, which is reflected in his works. He never dodged difficult questions, but often would mention that his conclusions were not the last word on the topic. He tackled the difficult subjects: his wife's painful illness and premature death, the problem of evil versus a good God, heaven, hell, miracles, the question if all or some will be "saved," and many others. Lewis most often centered his writings around the essentials of faith that unite all Christians, not on the issues that divide. He called himself a "mere Christian"[15]; he belonged to no camp or faction. He was not a "liberal," or a "fundamentalist," or an "evangelical." This non-alignment to a religious group has greatly enhanced his reputation, especially today.

C. S. Lewis's life is especially appealing because he was a convert in the truest sense. As a person who came to the faith only after years of thought and struggle, he certainly knew what it was to doubt and to have questions. As Lyle Dorsett wrote, Lewis

> knew the doubts of the people he hoped to reach. He asked their questions; he spoke their post-Christian language; he understood their emptiness; he knew from experience what might awaken them.[16]

In a recent book Alan Jones wrote about a discussion in which a student told him she had "the right to her opinion." Jones replied to her that her opinion was worthless because she had not thought about the subject and "made an effort to be informed."[17] One particular reason Lewis's opinions are listened to today is that he did think about his faith, and he did make an effort to be informed. He read; he argued; he debated; he asked questions; he almost literally "thought himself" into the Christian faith. C. S. Lewis "worked out his own salvation" as much as anyone ever did.

Other reasons have been given for Lewis's success and effectiveness: Americans are fascinated with the British (especially with British intellectuals), his lack of pretentiousness, the fact that he married an American rather late in his life, the fact that he was a spiritual mentor/guide to many persons through his letters, and because he wrote well in many literary (and Christian) genres.[18]

Perhaps the best way to sum up Lewis's effectiveness comes from one who knew him very well. Cecil Harwood was a lifelong friend whose influence on Lewis is mentioned in *Surprised by Joy*. In 1975, Harwood wrote these words about his friend:

> Indeed he opened windows for many people into realms hitherto unknown to them. No doubt he would have felt his greatest achievement was to open the windows of Christianity in a way no one else had done in his generation . . . He has indeed opened windows for us all, or we would not be here.[19]

## Prayer

The renowned preacher and theologian Austin Farrer believed that the most praiseworthy characteristic of his friend C. S. Lewis was that "Lewis could think about all that he strongly felt, and feel the realities about which he thought."[20] One aspect of the Christian life Lewis often thought about was prayer, and the realities of his own prayer life permeated his life and writings. After he became a Christian, he developed a well-reasoned and extraordinary prayer life, and this feature of his "life at the center" is a great key to his effectiveness and appeal to readers of all ages. Lyle Dorsett noted that prayer was the underlying factor in Lewis's strength and persistence in touching his readers' spirituality.[21]

In *Letters to Malcolm*, Lewis wrote to his fictitious friend Malcolm: "But however needed a good book on prayer is, I shall never try to write it."[22] I don't know if he was being tongue-in-cheek here or not, but he was genuinely and passionately interested in prayer throughout his life, both in theory and in practice. This interest reveals itself not only in his last Christian book, *Letters to Malcolm*, but in several other essays, poems, and longer passages in books, and in numerous letters to friends.[23]

Richard Harries wrote that Lewis would have certainly agreed with the statement, "to believe is to pray, and to cease to pray is to cease to believe."[24] Prayer for Lewis was many things: petitions for others, confession of sin, the worship and adoration of God, the enjoyment of the mystery and presence of God. As a believer and follower of God as revealed in Jesus Christ, he knew that prayer was the "attitude of the heart" that would always keep him close to his God.

Lewis once wrote that after he became a Christian, the best service he could do for people outside the faith was "to explain and defend the belief that has been common to nearly all Christians at all times."[25] Prayer supplied him with much of the spiritual energy to do that, and we are still seeing the results in lives all over the world.

## Devotion

C. S. Lewis cared deeply for the Bible, as will be obvious to anyone who carefully reads his works and/or books about his life. In addition to *Reflections on the Psalms*, he discussed in many books, essays, and letters various aspects of the Bible and biblical scholarship. He wrote about the Bible as literature, the inspiration of the Bible, ways of biblical interpretation, translations of the Bible, and Bible scholars. He also wrote about biblical themes such as miracles, heaven, Satan, hell, the atonement of Christ, the second coming of Christ, the resurrection of Christ, baptism, the Eucharist, sin, salvation, and the nature of God.[26]

As a Christian apologist or "defender of the faith," Lewis knew that there was danger in relying too heavily on reasonable argument to present his case for Christianity. He wrote, "We apologists . . . can be saved only by falling back . . . from Christian apologetics into Christ himself."[27] One way that Lewis "fell back into Christ" was in his devotion to Holy Scripture. For him, the Bible was a vehicle that continually carried him to Christ, and for this reason he read and studied it his entire Christian life.

Lewis knew that the Bible, if read in the right spirit, would carry the word of God to its reader. Scripture changed his life with that word of salvation and faith, so he always approached it with hope, knowledge, and openness. His life is a testimony to the fact that the Bible did change him for the better.

## Friendship

C. S. Lewis is unique among Christian contemporary thinkers in that he devoted so much of his attention to the theme of friendship; certainly it was very important to him throughout his life.[28] In 1941, he remarked in a letter to his friend Dom Bede Griffiths, "Is there any pleasure on earth as great as a circle of Christian friends by a good fire?"[29] Owen Barfield, Arthur Greeves, and Jack's brother, Warren, were all lifelong friends. Friendship was the basic ingredient of the Inklings, which included Christians such as Charles Williams, Nevil Coghill, J. R. R. Tolkien ("Tollers"), and H. V. D. ("Hugo") Dyson. The latter two were instrumental in Lewis's own conversion.

Jack also had several long and satisfying friendships with women, contrary to the advertisements for the movie *Shadowlands* that pictured him as sheltered. He lectured often at St. Mary's Convent, Wantage (near Oxford), and became good friends with the nuns there and with Sister Penelope Lawson. In Joy Davidman Gresham, Lewis had not only a wife, but a good and valued friend as well, a friend whom many people had a hard time accepting.

Lewis and the acclaimed poet Ruth Pitter were also close friends for many years; he had been instrumental in her own conversion to Christianity. And there were others, including Jane McNeil, a family friend; and Maureen Moore, the daughter of his "surrogate mother," Mrs. Janie King Moore (Jack "adopted" the Moores after the death of Janie's son during World War I). Lewis became friends with many women through his ministry of letter writing. One was Mary Willis Shelbourne, the "American Lady" of the book *Letters to an American Lady*. Other female friends were Kathryn Lindskoog, Jane Douglass, Dorothy L. Sayers, and a host of former students and admirers.

I have had the privilege of visiting Lewis's Oxford twice in the 1990s. On both trips I spent a few hours at the "Bird and Baby" pub, which is in the St. Giles district of the "city centre" of Oxford. On the walls of the back room where the Inklings met there are pictures of Lewis and his friends. Joy's picture is there, as are Dyson's and Tolkien's and Warren's and many more. I was struck by the impact that Lewis's friends made on his life. Lewis loved his friends, and they loved him. His friends were spiritually important to him, not only for their Christian companionship, but also for their prayers, advice, and interests shared.

He believed that his friendships provided him with the chief happiness of his life. He once wrote that friendship is something that raises people above humanity and is "eminently spiritual, the sort of love one can imagine among angels."[30] His friendships were an integral part of his "life at the center," and without them his life would have been much the poorer, and not even close to the angels.

## Notes

[1]Clifford Morris, "Portrait of C. S. Lewis," audio tape, Voyage to Narnia Lifestyle Courses (Elgin IL: David C. Cook, 1978).

[2]For more about heaven in Lewis's thought and works, see Wayne Martindale, ed., *Journey to the Celestial City* (Chicago: Moody Press, 1995) 129-43; and Kathryn Lindskoog, *C. S. Lewis: Mere Christian* (Downers Grove IL: InterVarsity Press, 1981) 79-88.

[3]Walter Hooper, ed., *They Stand Together: The Letters of C. S. Lewis to Arthur Greeves* (New York: Macmillan Press, 1979) 135.

[4]Ibid.

[5]*Time*, 8 September 1947, 65.

[6]Corbin Scott Carnell, *Bright Shadow of Reality: C. S. Lewis and the Feeling Intellect* (Grand Rapids MI: Eerdmans, 1974) 74.

[7]See "Memoir of C. S. Lewis," in W. H. Lewis, *Letters of C. S. Lewis*, revised edition edited by Walter Hooper (Orlando FL: Harcourt Brace, 1993) 36.

[8]Christopher Derrick, "Some Personal Memories of C. S. Lewis, an Incarnational Man," *New Oxford Review* (November 1987): 16-20.

[9]William Griffin, *Clive Staples Lewis: A Dramatic Life* (New York: Harper & Row, 1986) 253.

[10]John Lawlor, "The Tutor and Scholar," *Light on C. S. Lewis*, ed. Jocelyn Gibb (New York: Harcourt Brace, 1965) 73.

[11]Jill Freud, "Lewis Teaches the Retarded," *The Canadian C. S. Lewis Journal* (April 1980): 3-5.

[12]Edmund Crispin, *Swan Song* (New York: Avon Books, 1981) 62.

[13]John Wain, *Sprightly Running* (New York: St. Martin's Press, 1963) 184.

[14]Of the many editions of *A Grief Observed*, I recommend the version with a foreword by Madeleine L'Engle and the version with an afterword by Chad Walsh as being especially helpful to the general reader.

[15]The term "mere Christian" was used by the Puritan divine, Richard Baxter (1615–1691).

[16]Lyle W. Dorsett, "C. S. Lewis: Some Keys to His Effectiveness," Michael H. MacDonald and Andrew A. Tadie, eds., *The Riddle of Joy* (Grand Rapids MI: Eerdmans, 1989) 215-25.

[17]Alan Jones, *The Soul's Journey* (San Francisco: HarperCollins, 1995) 180.

[18]See also Richard L. Purtill, *C. S. Lewis's Case for the Christian Faith* (San Francisco: Harper & Row, 1981) 1-11; and Alan Jacobs, "The Second Coming of C. S. Lewis," *First Things* (November 1994): 27-30.

[19]"C. S. Lewis, A Toast," Owen Barfield, ed., *The Voice of Cecil Harwood* (London: Rudolf Steiner Press, 1979) 295.

[20]Charles C. Hefling, Jr., *Jacob's Ladder: Theology and Spirituality in the Thought of Austin Farrer* (Cambridge MA: Cowley Publications, 1979) 8.

[21]Dorsett, 218.

[22]C. S. Lewis, *Letters to Malcolm: Chiefly on Prayer* (New York: Harcourt, Brace, and World, 1964) 63.

[23]See Appendix C for a listing of Lewis's books and other writings that are about or have substantial sections on prayer.

[24]Richard Harries, *C. S. Lewis: The Man and His God* (Wilton CT: Morehouse-Barlow, 1987) 63.

[25]C. S. Lewis, *Mere Christianity* (London: Geoffrey Bles, 1952) vi.

[26]For reference guides to many of the quotes by Lewis on various aspects and themes of the Bible, see Wayne Martindale and Jerry Root, eds., *The Quotable C. S. Lewis* (Wheaton IL: Tyndale, 1989); and Clyde S. Kilby, ed., *A Mind Awake: An Anthology of C. S. Lewis* (New York: Harcourt Brace, 1968).

[27]C. S. Lewis, "Christian Apologetics," *Undeceptions* (London: Geoffrey Bles, 1971) 76. This work was later published as *God in the Dock*.

[28]Colin Duriez, *The C. S. Lewis Handbook* (Grand Rapids MI: Baker, 1990) 65.

[29]Hooper, 363.

[30]C. S. Lewis, *The Four Loves* (Orlando FL: Harcourt & Brace, 1988) 77.

# Chapter 2

## "It's So Much Easier to Pray for a Bore than It Is to Go See Him"

While he was still a teenager, unanswered prayer was one of the reasons Jack turned away from organized religion, the church, and God. When his beloved mother was seriously ill with cancer (Jack was ten years-old), his prayers for her healing were answered "no." In his autobiography Lewis wrote: "I remembered what I had been taught; that prayers offered in faith would be granted . . . When nevertheless she died."[1] His prayers for delivery from his horrible boyhood schools went unanswered, as did his prayers for the safety of his friends in World War I.

Kathryn Lindskoog wrote that the young Jack had another problem with prayer: his own inattention. He had been taught in early childhood that he must think about what he was saying in prayer. He carried this to the extreme. As soon as he would end his prayers, his conscience would accuse him of having not concentrated well enough and make him start all over again. Lindskoog related,

> By the time he abandoned Christianity, every evening was cloaked in gloom because he so dreaded bedtime and the nightly struggle for supreme concentration. Prayer meant pain, defeat, and much lost sleep.[2]

So he gradually gave up prayer, and Christianity with it.

After he became a Christian, Lewis learned that a mature prayer life is often nurtured by suffering. He suffered greatly because his best friend and brother, Warnie, was an alcoholic, even though Jack had counseled and prayed for him most of his adult life. Warnie was a Christian gentleman, a wonderful writer, and was very well-liked by everyone who knew him. His alcoholism led him to the point of hospitalization and even near death several times, however. Jack accepted this the best way he could. He knew that God's knowledge of our real needs and the way in which they can be satisfied far exceeded his own knowledge. He also knew that "God's ways are not our ways" and often seem unwise to human beings. So he was wise enough to give God his confidence, even though he could not understand God's "no answer" to his prayers for Warnie's deliverance.

Lewis also suffered a great deal because of the rejection of his own university. Through the years he encountered much opposition at Oxford, due primarily to his outspoken and emphatic Christian apologetic, and because he wrote popular Christian books for laypeople. Oxford never recognized his true worth and never offered him an academic chair or full professorship. When he moved from Magdalen College, Oxford, to a full professorship at Magdalene College, Cambridge, he wrote to a friend,

> I think I shall like Magdalene better than Magdalen . . . (here) they're so old-fashioned, and pious, and gentle, and conservative—unlike this leftist, atheist, cynical, hard-boiled, huge Magdalen.[3]

This career-long disappointment, and the suffering caused by it, hurt him deeply and reinforced his belief in prayer as the way to a God who never disappoints.

Near the end of his life, because of his marriage to Joy and her death, Lewis experienced the most profound happiness and deepest suffering he had yet known. Although some authors have written (inexplicably) that their marriage was one "of convenience," or even that Joy "duped" or "used" Jack, there is no doubt that they were in love. Once, while talking to his friend Nevil Coghill, Lewis remarked that he never expected to have in his sixties the happiness that had passed him by in his twenties.[4] In fact, his stepson, Douglas Gresham, said that his mother and Jack were supremely happy together; in fact "their marriage was the happiest time in both of their lives."[5]

After Joy died, however, Jack's faith in prayer was severely tested. In *A Grief Observed* he laments the fact that God was not there when God was so urgently needed:

> Where is God? . . . go to Him when your need is desperate . . . and what do you find? A door slammed in your face, and the sound of bolting and double bolting on the inside. After that silence.[6]

Some C. S. Lewis scholars have written that *A Grief Observed* really shows that Jack lost his faith in God, but the book is actually one-third grief and two-thirds recovery. Jack's problem was that when his prayers of grief were not answered immediately, he believed God to be cruel and unjust: "I am not in much danger of ceasing to believe in God. The real danger is of coming to believe such dreadful things about him."[7] Lewis finally came to see that his prayers were heard by a loving God, and that God's timetable of helping him was there all the time—he had to "let go" and give all to God, even his struggling prayers.

A Baptist layperson once asked me if Lewis had a "theology of prayer." I told her that the two features of prayer he stressed the most in his writings and asked the most questions about were concerned with the nature of intercessory prayer (prayers for others) and the effectiveness of prayer (how does prayer actually work). In most of his books and articles about prayer Lewis wrote about his own struggles and questions.

*Letters to Malcolm: Chiefly on Prayer* was published just six months after his death. In it Lewis pretends to be comparing notes with a friend about prayer and all of its problems. There are personal comments about prayer in *Surprised by Joy* and *The Screwtape Letters*, and *Miracles* has a chapter that examines the role of prayer in the providential nature of God. *Letters to an American Lady* is a much underrated collection of letters to a lady with many problems. Throughout his writings we can see glimpses of Jack's own faithful prayer life.

He published an article called "The Efficacy of Prayer" that gives his views on how prayers actually are answered. In this essay, just after a poignant little section about his wife's seemingly miraculous recovery from cancer, Lewis adds,

> But once again there is no rigorous proof (that prayer "caused" the miracle) . . . The question then arises, "What sort of evidence would prove the efficacy (effectiveness) of prayer?"[8]

*Christian Reflections* contains an essay called "Petitionary Prayer: A Problem Without an Answer," which is an address Lewis gave to a group of ministers in 1953. The article "Work and Prayer," in *God in the Dock*, answers questions about prayer. In the essay "Scraps," also in *God in the Dock*, Lewis ponders the question of asking God for particular things when God already knows what is best for us.

Even after he matured and became a Christian, he had to work very hard at prayer. And "saying one's prayers" was for him only a small part of his total experience of prayer. He sometimes prayed without using words. In his petitionary prayers he would substitute mental images of the people he was praying for instead of saying their names.

Lewis learned to develop a "practical rhythm" of prayer. He would usually rise about 7:00 A.M., take a walk, attend matins (a time of daily prayer) at 8:00 A.M. in his college chapel, have breakfast, and start his tutorials and lectures about 9:00 A.M. Late in most afternoons he would make time for prayerful thought and contemplation as he walked the college grounds. He tried not to pray just before he went to bed at night. He believed that praying while tired or sleepy was the worst possible time to pray, due to problems of concentration. Instead, he would pray on a train while traveling, or walk and pray behind the train station while waiting.

Douglas Gresham wrote that prayer for his stepfather did indeed become a faithful practice, one that he adhered to as a daily routine:

> I remember that he spent much time in prayer. He had his own regular prayer times, both morning and evening, but was often to be found in prayer at any time during the day. I think that when a question or issue turned up that required prayer . . . Jack wasted no time but turned at once to the Lord.[9]

Jack's close friend and biographer, George Sayer, mentioned that Lewis "of course talked to God at all sorts of times in the day. I don't think he ever quite ceased to have mystical experiences, those of JOY."[10]

For many years after his conversion, during his private devotional times Jack would pray the Lord's Prayer—"a ready-made prayer"—in combination with his own words—which he called "festoons." Festoons were the very personal "private grace notes" on which he "liked to hang on the basic petitions" of our Lord's Prayer.[11] These "grace notes" helped him give additional meanings to the Lord's Prayer and made it easier to pray. For instance, he would festoon the phrase "hallowed be thy name" with the words "with angels and archangels and all the company of heaven."[12] To "thy will be done," he would add the festoon "thy will be *done*—by me—now."[13] Using festoonings in prayer was Lewis's way of combining reverence before God with honesty and humility about his own life. With this type of prayer he learned that real communication with God is both general and specific.

Lewis's biggest problem with prayer was that the Bible seems to instruct us to pray in two mutually exclusive ways. He devoted most of his writings on prayer to this problem and sought the answer to it for years. The first way is the way of Christ in Gethsemane, the way of submission to God's will. This was usually Lewis's pattern in prayer. The second way is that of "sure expectation." Lewis believed that several Bible passages clearly seem to promise that requests will be granted if prayed for in faith. For example, he always prayed that his friends' illnesses might be healed "if it was God's will."

In an address to a group of ministers concerning the problems of petitionary prayer, Lewis said that he had taken this problem to almost every Christian layperson and minister he knew in the Church of England and had received no answer.[14] At the end of his ten-page talk, he asked his listeners for help: "How am I to pray this very night?"[15] It is not recorded if he received an answer from anyone in the group who heard him.

In *Letters to Malcolm* Lewis concludes that for most Christians, Jesus' prayer in Gethsemane is the only model.[16] For him, the main conflict was to believe that, whether God will grant them or not, God listens to our prayers and takes them seriously. He admitted that there are unresolved problems concerning prayer, and that the biblical promises about the granting of prayers require faith that most believers never experience. He also saw that often the "great" Christians seemed to receive fewer answers than did new or "beginning" Christians.

Still, Lewis was not naive about petitionary prayer. In *Letters to Malcolm* he shows his sense of humor and balanced approach to the Christian life when he wrote about combining prayer with real action on the behalf of others:

> I too had noticed that our prayers for others flow more easily than those we offer on our behalf . . . I am often, I

believe, praying for others when I should be doing things for them. It's so much easier to pray for a bore than to go and see him.[17]

Lewis learned that one's feelings for people should not interfere with an obedient routine of prayer. In a letter to his friend and former student Dom Bede Griffiths he admitted that praying with love for villains such as Hitler and Stalin was very difficult, but nevertheless should be done. To help him do this, he remembered that in personal prayer one joins Christ's perpetual intercession for all the human race. He also recalled his own dark side, which "might have blossomed under different conditions into something terrible."[18]

This same theme is echoed in Letter Four of *The Screwtape Letters*, where Screwtape advises his pupil Wormwood to misdirect the "patient" from real prayer to vaguely devotional moods and feelings. Walter Hooper and Owen Barfield, authors of a study guide on Lewis's famous classic, commented that "while prayer is invaluable and commanded of us, it is disastrously easy to think it all really depends on our feelings."[19]

Like many Christians, C. S. Lewis learned to pray routinely when he was depressed or having spiritual difficulties. He also learned that prayer was just difficult even in the best of times. He wrote about the challenge of having an ordered prayer life, and how this was so hard to achieve even when things were going very well:

> Prayer is irksome. An excuse to omit it is never unwelcome . . . We are reluctant to begin. We are delighted to finish . . . The odd thing is that this reluctance to pray is not confined to periods of dryness. When yesterday's prayers were full of comfort and exhaltation, today's will still be felt as, in some degree, a burden.[20]

Lewis recognized this problem his entire life. He often asked his friends to pray for him more when everything was well with him. In a letter to his friend Sister Penelope Lawson he wrote:

> I specially need your prayers because I am (like the pilgrim in Bunyan) traveling across "a plain called Ease."

Everything without and many things within are marvelously
well at present.[21]

In her excellent treatment of Lewis's life of prayer,
Kathryn Lindskoog noted that Jack had enough "yes" answers
to his prayers to fill him with awe many times.[22] On one occasion he had a compulsion to go to the barber, although he did
not need a haircut that day—he had always hated getting
haircuts and considered them a bother. When he entered the
shop, the barber told him that he had a terrible problem and
had been praying for Lewis to come see him.

Another time a minister friend, Peter Bide, had laid hands
on Joy Lewis as she lay dying, and had prayed for her healing.
At the same time of the healing prayer, Lewis himself prayed a
prayer of "substitution" for her—that she would be healed
and, if possible, her illness be given to him. Almost immediately, Joy started healing, and the cancerous spots started
disappearing from her bones. Soon after that, Lewis developed
osteoporosis, a bone disease that plagued him for the rest of
his life. Although Joy suffered a relapse three years later, and
Lewis knew that she might have healed even without the
prayers, he always marveled at the timing of the prayers and
the healing.

In a recent devotional work Thomas Moore wrote percep-
tively that "prayer cleanses us of expectations and allows holy
will, providence, and life itself an entry."[23] During his earthly
pilgrimage Jack Lewis fought many hard battles with the
problem of prayer and came up with many answers and
reflections . . . and sometimes more problems. Yet his last
words in the last book he wrote before he died were about
heaven.

He wrote often about heaven, and for Jack, heaven was
the perfect ending to a book about prayer. Prayer became for
him a revelation *of* God and a pathway *to* God, a pathway that
was leading to heaven. As his life went on, the questions and
answers and problems of prayer became less important.

Perhaps it is fitting to close this chapter about Lewis and
prayer with his words spoken to that group of ministers in
1953:

In it (prayer) God shows Himself to us. That he answers
prayer is a corollary—not necessarily the most important
one—from the revelation. What (God) does is learned from
what (God) is.[24]

## Notes

[1]C. S. Lewis, *Surprised by Joy* (Orlando FL: Harcourt Brace,
1984) 20.

[2]Kathryn Lindskoog, *C. S. Lewis: Mere Christian* (Downers
Grove IL: InterVarsity Press, 1981) 117-18.

[3]William Griffin, *Clive Staples Lewis: A Dramatic Life* (New
York: Harper & Row, 1986) 356.

[4]Roger Lancelyn Green and Walter Hooper, *C. S. Lewis: A
Biography* (New York: Harcourt Brace, 1974) 270.

[5]Douglas Gresham, conversation with author, Nashville,
Tennessee, 16 August 1995.

[6]C. S. Lewis, *A Grief Observed* (San Francisco: Harper & Row,
1989) 18.

[7]Ibid.

[8]C. S. Lewis, *The World's Last Night and Other Essays* (New
York: Harcourt Brace, 1960) 4.

[9]Douglas Gresham, letter to author, 26 April 1995.

[10]George Sayer, letter to author, 18 May 1995. Note: "JOY"
(from the German *sehnsucht,* "longing") is the term Lewis used to
describe authentic experiences with God. For a lucid and well-written account of "joy" in Lewis's life, see Corbin Scott Carnell, *Bright
Shadow of Reality: C. S. Lewis and the Feeling Intellect* (Grand
Rapids MI: Eerdmans, 1974).

[11]Perry LeFevre, *Understandings of Prayer* (Philadelphia:
Westminster, 1981) 113.

[12]C. S. Lewis, *Letters*, 15.

[13]Ibid, 26.

[14]C. S. Lewis, "Petitionary Prayer: A Problem Without an
Answer," address to the Oxford Clerical Society, 8 December 1953.

[15]C. S. Lewis, *Christian Reflections*, Walter Hooper, ed. (Grand
Rapids MI: Eerdmans, 1967) 142-51.

[16]C. S. Lewis, *Letters*, 60.

[17]Ibid, 66.

[18]W. H. Lewis, *Letters of C. S. Lewis*, revised edition edited by
Walter Hooper (Orlando FL: Harcourt Brace, 1993), 347.

[19]Walter Hooper and Owen Barfield, *A Study Guide to The Screwtape Letters* (West Chicago IL: Lord and King Associates, 1976) 114. See also Frank S. Kastor, *C. S. Lewis—A Study Guide: The Screwtape Letters* (Wichita KS: St. Mark's Press, 1994).

[20]C. S. Lewis, *Letters*, 113.

[21]W. H. Lewis, *Letters*, 410.

[22]Lindskoog, *C. S. Lewis: Mere Christian*, 120.

[23]Thomas Moore, *Meditations* (New York: HarperCollins, 1994) 19.

[24]C. S. Lewis, *The World's Last Night*, 8.

# Chapter 3

## "The Bible, Read in the Right Spirit . . . Will Bring Us to God"

## The Gospel Stories and Lewis's Conversion

The Bible was not a part of C. S. Lewis's childhood. Although his parents taught him to say prayers at bedtime and sent him to church regularly, there is no record of young Jack "being taught the Bible" when he was a little boy. Albert and Flora Lewis were good people and good parents, but were rather nominal Christians. In his autobiography, *Surprised by Joy*, Lewis remembers that his father's approach to religion was "high" (rigid and fundamentalistic), and of his mother's faith he can remember nothing. Thus, for C. S. Lewis, the Bible became a "late and acquired taste."[1]

He was introduced to the Bible at age ten after his mother's death and also after he was sent to Wynyard, a boys "prep" school in Watford, between Oxford and London. There he attended church twice every Sunday, heard doctrinal sermons preached, and started reading the Bible for the first time in his life. He gradually lost whatever faith he had as a teenager and became a confirmed (and arrogant) atheist for nearly twenty years.

There are many well-documented reasons why Lewis rejected Christianity. One of the strongest was the fact that his private tutor for Oxford, W. T. Kirkpatrick ("the Great Knock"), reinforced Lewis's growing contempt for people who could believe in God without rational evidence. Kirkpatrick taught Jack to think and to use logic, but also to believe strongly that "the pathway to truth" came *only* through reason, not through any religion, or faith, or reliance upon "the Bible"—or any bible.

When Lewis became a tutor at Magdalen College at Oxford, his ideas about the Bible began to change gradually. At first he saw the Christian religion as "man-made" (like all the others), Jesus as a Jewish philosopher with a cult following, and the miracles described in the Bible as legends. Over a period of years, and after many agonizing talks and arguments with students and friends—many of whom were Christians—he began to see the Bible in a different light.

He started reading books about religion, some of which confirmed his atheism, while others disturbed it. As he studied and read and thought, Lewis came to notice what he later called "holiness" in friends and fellow scholars such as J. R. R. Tolkien, Owen Barfield, Nevil Coghill, and "Hugo" Dyson. He reread Christian authors whom he had read previously because of their literary abilities: G. K. Chesterton, George MacDonald, and Jacob Boehme, for example.

Several events and factors pushed Lewis toward conversion (first to theism, then to Christianity) and a new understanding of the Bible. Perhaps the most significant event was a conversation he had with a "hard-boiled" atheist (a well-known philosopher) at his college who reluctantly admitted that there was good evidence for the historicity of the Gospel accounts of Jesus. Further, this man stated that the recurring presence of stories of dying and resurrected gods in the ancient folklore and traditions of ancient peoples also suggested that the Gospel stories were true, particularly about Jesus' death and resurrection.

Lewis began to examine the evidence for Christ on his own and had to agree that it was "surprisingly good." He kept remembering Chesterton's words from his great book *The Everlasting Man*, that in claiming to be the Son of God, Jesus Christ was either a maniac or a blasphemer or he was speaking the truth.[2] His problem with the Gospel accounts of Jesus' life, death, and resurrection had always been that they were just part of the whole pantheon of "sacrifice tales" that permeate history. He believed that the Gospel "myths" were like all the others.

After dinner one night in 1931, he and his friends Hugo Dyson and J. R. R. Tolkien took a long stroll around Addison's Walk, the beautiful and secluded path around the deer park near where Lewis lived at Magdalen. Dyson and Tolkien engaged Lewis in a long discussion about history and myth, a talk that was probably the turning point for him. The two friends convinced Jack that the pagan myths of dying and reviving gods did not prove that the Christ story in the Gospels is false. On the contrary, the ancient stories show how pagan peoples had a glimpse of the truth that was going to happen and in fact did happen 2,000 years ago in Jesus the Christ. A few weeks after this talk, Lewis wrote to his friend Arthur Greeves,

> Now the story of Christ is simply a true myth: a myth working on us as the same way as the others, but with this tremendous difference, that it really happened.[3]

Lewis started reading the Bible again, particularly the Gospels and especially the Gospel of Mark. He began to be aware that the Gospel accounts were not untrue myths or made-up stories, because their authors used such plain, honest language and did not attempt to be overly imaginative. He read the psalms avidly and became an admirer of these poems for life. Lewis's first biographers noted that Lewis had already begun reading the Gospel of John in Greek, "thus initiating a practice he was to continue for the rest of his life: to read some portion of the Bible almost every day."[4]

### How Lewis Approached the Bible

In the 1950s, the American scholars Corbin Carnell and Clyde S. Kilby wrote to C. S. Lewis asking him what he thought about the Bible generally, the inspiration of the Bible, and the Bible as history. A summary of his replies to them are worth noting:

- The Bible is inspired.
- The different literary genres (allegory, parable, romance, lyric, and so on) are just as inspired as the chronicles ("historical stories").
- The books of Jonah and Esther are "moral romances"—in the literary sense, stories that entertain with an ethical overtone—and that to question their historicity does not lead one logically to question the validity of the New Testament miracles.
- The inconsistencies of some biblical passages, particularly the genealogies of Matthew 1 and Luke 3 and the two different accounts of Judas's death in Matthew 27:5 and Acts 1:18-19, rule out the view that every statement in the Bible *must* be "historical" truth.
- By their nature, some passages in the Bible seem to be differently inspired than others.

- All specific scripture texts cannot be assumed to be "inner-ant" in the same sense as others—scripture must be evaluated in its context.
- The primary function of the Bible is to convey God's word to the reader, who must be "inspired" and who will read in the right spirit.[5]

Lewis never worked out a systematic approach to the nature of scripture, which is understandable, since he never claimed to be a systematic theologian, nor was he a "lay theologian" as some say. A fact that seems almost comical is that "fundamentalists," "conservatives," "liberals," and "evangelicals" all claim that Lewis belongs to them—at least as far as the Bible is concerned. He believed that the Bible was inspired by God, but that not every part of it was equally inspired. And he never limited God's inspiration to the Scriptures alone. He believed that God also revealed Himself in literature, other religions, myths, reason, nature, art, and music.

Any Christian writer who achieves popular acclaim inevitably becomes controversial. Lewis was no exception. Some scholars have said that his approach to the Bible offers a middle ground between radicalism and literalism. Consequently, he cannot really please "liberals" or "conservatives." Because he believed in miracles and that the New Testament is historically accurate, the "liberals" of his day accused him of being a fundamentalist. Because he recognized many problem areas of scripture and faced them straightforwardly, some "fundamentalists" and "conservatives" of his day accused him of theological liberalism.

He admitted frankly that the Bible contains some errors and distorted ideas. He understood the story of Adam and Eve mythically; today he might be called a "theistic evolutionist." He believed in the biblical heaven and hell, but being true to his Anglican heritage, he also believed in purgatory as a place for the "cleansing of the soul." In *The Problem of Pain* he suggests the possibility that animals might be immortal. He questioned whether Job, Jonah, Esther, and Ruth were historical or not. He was troubled by the "cursing" psalms, and he wrote that he often struggled to hear God's word through the pessimism of Ecclesiastes.

If you read C. S. Lewis carefully, however, you will not get the impression of a man who "sits on the fence" as regards the basic message of the Bible. He believed that many of the clergy of his day went too far in interpreting the Bible metaphorically, such as when Christ told his disciples to take up the cross. He felt that too many ministers and scholars wrongly concluded that carrying the cross meant nothing more than leading a "respectable" life and giving to charitable causes. He knew that some thought hell and heaven were "states of mind"; he had strong words for them. And Lewis had quite a bit to say to those who "watered down the Bible" and tried to strip it of its obvious meaning—whether intentionally or unintentionally—for instance, those who believed that God was not personal but "a great spiritual force" or a "perfect substance." For these people, Lewis wrote with his usual candor and humor:

> A girl I knew was brought up to regard God as a perfect "substance"; in later life she realized that this had actually led her to think of Him as something like a vast tapioca pudding. (To make matters worse, she disliked tapioca.)[6]

He later added that no person is safe from this kind of absurd metaphorical thinking about the Bible.

Lewis cannot be held to any one position concerning Holy Scripture. For him, the Bible was not a systematic theology or a doctrinal primer or denominational handbook. But his love for the Bible was such that he compared it to Jesus. He observed that Jesus' perfect teachings were not given to us in book form or in a cut-and-dried foolproof, systematic fashion. Lewis wrote:

> We have only reported sayings, most of them uttered in answer to questions shaped in some degree by their context. And when we have collected them all we cannot reduce them to a system.[7]

And in a letter to a friend, Lewis warned against interpreting the Bible in a way that Jesus would come off second best:

> We must not interpret any one part of scripture so that it contradicts other parts, and specially we must not use an apostle's teaching to contradict that of our Lord.[8]

So how did Lewis approach the Bible? He wrote that the Bible "is fundamentally a sacred book and demands to be taken on its own terms."[9] He thought that we should not use it as an encyclopedia of systematic truth, but rather live in it by "steeping ourselves in its tone and temper and so learn its overall message."[10] For Lewis, biblical truth was dynamic, changing. He said that the moment we try to abstract or systematize the Bible, we lose its essence.

Lewis wrote one book about the Bible: *Reflections on the Psalms*. After it appeared, he was asked to serve as one of the seven members of the committee to revise the psalms for the Church of England. The *Revised Psalter* is not often listed as one of Lewis's books; but he, T. S. Eliot, and others "modernized" the old Coverdale translation for *The Book of Common Prayer*. He also was consulted about various points of translation in the New Testament section of the New English Bible.

For some reason, *Reflections on the Psalms*, while being a steady seller through the years, has not achieved the popularity of Lewis's other works. His friend Austin Farrer suggested that he write the book. It came at a time when Lewis was worried about Joy Gresham's illness and his own poor health. Farrer and Joy both told him there was a great need for a book that would deal with the things that worried people when they read the psalms. In fact, Joy helped him edit and type the book. *Reflections on the Psalms* was criticized by some scholars for "not being a work of scholarship," yet Lewis wrote in the introduction that it was not meant to be a work of scholarship! He prefaced the book by saying,

> I write as one amateur to another, talking about difficulties I
> have met, or lights that I have gained . . . I am comparing
> notes, not presuming to instruct.[11]

The first few chapters of *Reflections* deal with the aspects of the psalms that repel many "modern" readers: the way they welcome the day of judgment, the frequent cursings, their delight in the slaughter of the enemies of Israel, the lack of belief in a life after death, and their sometimes self-righteousness. Despite these problem areas, most of the book contains personal descriptions of the pleasure Lewis received from reading the psalms. "The most valuable things the psalms do for me is to express the same delight in God which made David dance." Lewis talked about the pleasure one gets from using the psalms in church as a great aid in worship, the way they often are prayers for us when we cannot say the words, and their obvious "gusto" or appetite for God. He wrote of the beauty of God's law and the way in which the psalms revel in it. He loved the way the psalms rejoice in nature and in all of God's creation, which is good. He also discussed the psalms as great poetry and introduced the reader to meter, structure, and form.

In the chapter called "Scripture," toward the end of the book, Lewis "sums up" his thoughts about the Bible. These are some of the most beautiful words he ever wrote, and again he takes the reader back to Jesus:

> Taken by a literalist, He (Jesus) will always prove to be the most elusive of teachers. Systems cannot keep up with that darting illumination. No net less wide than a man's whole heart, nor less fine a mesh as love, will hold the sacred Fish.[12]

Lewis believed that everyone should read the Bible and receive the message of scripture and the "sacred Fish," or Christ, with the "net of love," which is the "affirming embrace" of the Word of God. The "mesh" is a person's whole heart; so for Lewis, faith required the total, passionate response of the whole person—what the Bible demands.

Jack Lewis was devoted to the Bible. He did not worship it, but he did "steep himself in it" and tried to follow its basic message his entire Christian life. For him, the Bible was at the center of his spirituality. He fervently believed that the fundamental purpose of the Bible is to convey God's word to the reader . . . and that word starts with Jesus.

## How C. S. Lewis Read the Bible

A person's "devotional life" is a private matter between that person and God. It is not surprising that we do not have much information on how Lewis actually read the Bible when he was alone. What we do know can shed some light on him as an obedient disciple of Christ, and that obedience can be an example for anyone who wishes to hear.

After Lewis became a Christian, he tried to read a passage from the Bible devotionally nearly every day. He would read a passage from Psalms, followed by one from the Gospels or Paul's writings. When traveling on a train, he would sometimes read from the Greek New Testament or *The Book of Common Prayer*. Lewis recommended reading works in their original language, the "primary source." Since he had a good knowledge of biblical Hebrew, and used it (transliterated) in some of his works, it is a safe assumption that he probably read from the Hebrew Bible as well. He also read the New Testament in Latin, as he stated in a letter to a friend rather whimsically:

> By the way good easy Latin reading to keep one's Latin up with is the New Testament in Latin . . . say you want a copy of the Vulgate (VULGATE) New Testament. *Acts* goes specially well in Latin.[13]

Those who knew C. S. Lewis have testified about his steadfastness in reading the Bible on a daily basis. His friend and biographer, George Sayer, wrote that when Lewis visited him, he would return home after a walk about 6:00 P.M. (before the evening meal) and "read a passage from any translation of the Bible and say his prayers."[14] Sayer also wrote, "I know his formal periods of prayer as often as possible began with the reading of a chapter or some verses of the Bible."[15] Douglas Gresham added,

> I remember that Jack read at least a chapter (sometimes far more depending on available time) of the Bible every day. He read the Authorised Version, J. B. Phillips' New Testament translation, and the New Testament in the original Greek.[16]

Because of *Reflections on the Psalms*, we know that the Psalter had a special place in the heart of Lewis and that likely he read from it more often than any other book of the Bible. A specific favorite was from Psalms 119:1-24.

> Happy are those whose way is blameless, who walk in the law of the Lord. Happy are those who keep his decrees, who seek him with their whole heart, who also do no wrong, but walk in his ways. You have commanded your precepts to be

kept diligently. O that my ways may be steadfast in keeping
your statutes!

It is easy to see why Lewis loved this passage. With his lifelong
devotion to obedience and his desire "to do right" in everything he undertook, these verses exemplify him as a happy,
contented Christian who enjoyed the new life he had been
given by God.

The apostle Paul's famous words from a Philippian jail
could justly be described as Lewis's "credo":

> Work out your own salvation with fear and trembling; for it
> is God who is at work in you, enabling you both to will and
> to work for his good pleasure. (Phil 2:12-13)

For a man who traveled "the long road" from atheism to
theism, and finally to belief in Jesus as the Christ, this passage
is most appropriate. Lewis was always a seeker. If anyone ever
used the gifts God gave them to explore, ask questions, and
find answers with the whole heart and mind, it was Lewis.

Another significant passage from the New Testament for
him was 2 Corinthians 4:16-18. These words formed the textual basis for his famous sermon "The Weight of Glory." The
text reads:

> So we do not lose heart. Even though our outer nature is
> wasting away, our inner nature is being renewed day by day.
> For this slight momentary affliction is preparing us for an
> eternal weight of glory beyond all measure, because we look
> not at what can be seen but what cannot be seen; for what
> can be seen is temporary, but what cannot be seen is
> eternal.

Lewis said he wrote about heaven in nearly all his books.
The Corinthian passage is a great summation of the hope that
was always a "bright blur" for him. But Lewis was a person
who was grounded in reality. He knew there was much work
for him to do while he was on *this* earth. He knew that his
calling was to teach, to write, to be a spiritual mentor and
friend. That sure knowledge of the coming "weight of glory"
was a major part of his balanced life as a Christian. He knew
also that his belief in heaven was straight from Jesus and

straight from the Bible. His "life at the center" was real and
true because he immersed himself in the Bible every day.

## Notes

[1]C. S. Lewis, *Surprised by Joy* (Orlando FL: Harcourt Brace,
1984) 7-8.

[2]See G. K. Chesterton, "The Riddles of the Gospel," in *The
Everlasting Man* (Garden City NY: Image Books, 1955) 185-97.

[3]Walter Hooper, ed., *They Stand Together: The Letters of C. S.
Lewis to Arthur Greeves* (New York: Macmillan Press, 1979) 428.

[4]Walter Hooper and Roger Lancelyn Green, *C. S. Lewis: A
Biography* (New York: Harcourt Brace, 1974) 104.

[5]Michael J. Christensen, "Two Letters from C. S. Lewis," *C. S.
Lewis on Scripture* (Waco TX: Word, 1979) 97-99.

[6]C. S. Lewis, *Miracles: A Preliminary Study* (London: Geoffrey
Bles, 1947) 90.

[7]C. S. Lewis, *Reflections on the Psalms* (New York: Harcourt,
Brace and World, 1958) 112-13.

[8]W. H. Lewis, *Letters of C. S. Lewis*, revised edition edited by
Walter Hooper (Orlando FL: Harcourt Brace, 1993) Lewis, 432.

[9]C. S. Lewis, *They Asked for a Paper* (London: Geoffrey Bles,
1962) 48-49.

[10]C. S. Lewis, *Reflections*, 112.

[11]Ibid, 2.

[12]Ibid, 119.

[13]W. H. Lewis, *Letters*, 467.

[14]Stephen Schofield, ed., *In Search of C. S. Lewis* (South
Plainfield NJ: Bridge Publishing, 1983) 91.

[15]George Sayer, letter to author, 18 May 1995.

[16]Douglas Gresham, letter to author, 26 April 19.

# Chapter 4

"Is Any Pleasure on Earth
as Great as a Circle of Friends
by a Fire?"

# How C. S. Lewis Saw Friendship

A beautiful scene in the movie *Shadowlands* is that of Jack and Joy Lewis driving in the glorious Welsh countryside in a little yellow car. Something is wrong with that scene, however. Jack never learned to drive a car very well. He either walked or rode buses, taxis, and trains, or was chauffeured by friends and family. He came to rely on Clifford Morris of the Oxford Taxi Company as his good companion and driver for much of his later life. In a talk over the Oxford BBC after Lewis's death, Morris paid this tribute to his friend, with words that exemplify what real friendship meant to C. S. Lewis:

> Dr. Lewis was a man to whom one would go (to) and be sure that one would receive *all that could possibly be given* of Christian love, understanding, and helpfulness . . . he was one of the most approachable men I have ever met.[1]

Other than his letters, much of what Lewis wrote about friendship is contained in *The Four Loves*. In this book, Lewis discusses the four major Greek words for love, two of which are found in the New Testament. Lewis believed that friendship (*philia*) was a type or form of love, just like affection (*storge*) or married love (*eros*). These three Lewis called the "natural" (human) loves, and none of them could prosper without God's love (*agape*).

Lewis's way of looking at friendship was different from most. For him, friendship (*philia*) was not just "companionship" or "fellowship" or "clubability." Friendship has a spiritual, God-centered dimension to it. It arises out of and goes deeper than companionship. Lewis knew that for friendship to be truly spiritual, it had to be more than just "doing things together" or "being together." God-centered friends do "inward" things together as opposed to "outward" things. Kathryn Lindskoog wrote that Lewis saw friendship "as about things like truth; they [friends] either see the same truth or care about the same truth. Their friendship is about something."[2]

Lewis also saw friendship as never being self-serving. A true friend will always help when needed, but a true friend will never look for thanks or gratitude or dependence. Friendship for Lewis never looked at "class" differences; he considered race, income, and family background as incidental to the friendship itself. In *The Four Loves* he shows his always abiding interest in heaven by comparing friendship with it. Since God-centered friendship can never be possessive, and real friends should always be willing to share each other, Lewis saw it as

> a glorious "nearness by resemblance" to heaven itself where the very multitude of the blessed . . . increases the fruition each has of God . . . the more we thus share of the Heavenly Bread between us, the more we shall have.[3]

A non-possessive friendship has in it the very essence of *community* (heaven); and the more friendships are shared, the more one will gain spiritually.

Lewis saw two weaknesses that can arise in a human friendship. It can either turn out to be a "school of virtue" or a "school of vice." In other words, friends, even when they have "deep things" in common, can come to feel that their shared views and interests—even when bad or evil—are best for everyone and cannot be disputed or open to change. This situation leads to another potential weakness of human friendship.

A friendship can become indifferent toward outside opinion and grow into a general disregard for *any* person not in the circle of friends. Lewis said this potential for group pride can lead to an exclusiveness that is the greatest danger of friendship. This is the opposite of community and leads to the opposite of heaven. Lewis's name for this type of dangerous friendship was the *inner* ring.[4] He believed that inner rings exist everywhere: in government, school, businesses, the church. The best friendship is the one that does not congratulate itself and enjoy its exclusiveness, but one that sees itself as a gift from God.

C. S. Lewis thought of Christian friendship as the "highest" of all friendships. He asked Christians to always remember that they have been chosen by God, and that friendships united by Christ are not rewards for our good taste or intelligent discrimination. Christian friendships are initiated by God to help humans discover what is good and beautiful in each one of them. Friendships of this type should strive to be positive and hopeful, but not take themselves too seriously. Lewis commented:

> Not that we must always partake of it solemnly. God who made good laughter forbid . . . we must deeply acknowledge certain things to be serious and yet retain the power and will to treat them often as lightly as a game.[5]

He wrote that friendship in the modern society of his day was not considered a "love" and had not been given the same value as eros or even storge. But for him, the survival of Christianity has depended on God-centered friendship, because "the little pockets of early Christians survived because they cared exclusively for the 'love of the brethren.' "[6] Because he really believed this, Jack saw his friends as friends for life.

## C. S. Lewis and His Friends: The Inklings

The Inklings have been described as "a group of male friends gathered around Jack Lewis because of their mutual enjoyment of good conversation and friendship."[7] It is reasonable to call the Inklings the most famous literary-Christian group of this generation. Their writings and influence upon the consciousness of the post-World War II generation has been enormous. Besides Jack Lewis, the group included J. R. R. Tolkien, Charles Williams, and his brother Warren ("Warnie") Lewis.

Other than close friendship (away from the group as well), the common threads that defined the group were its informality and shared interests. The Inklings were informal in that there was no "held membership," no initiation rites, no formal meetings, no rules, no officers, and no agenda. Yet the group did meet regularly for about twenty years, beginning around 1933 and ending between 1949 and 1955. The Inklings met on Tuesdays at the famous "Bird and Baby" pub in downtown Oxford, and then on Thursdays they would gather in Lewis's rooms at Magdalen College. They would discuss politics, books they were reading, religion, and various and sundry other topics.

Lewis was at his best during these times and often showed a human side that was far different from how he has been portrayed in recent films. Warnie wrote that Jack's talk at the Inklings meetings "was an outpouring of wit, nonsense, whimsy, dialectical swordplay, and pungent judgments."[8] The only structure to the meetings was that Lewis would insist upon the reading of manuscripts being written at the time by those attending. This was not a mutual admiration society when it came to criticism of the works that were read. Warnie wrote in his memoir: "Praise for good work was unstinted, but censure for bad work—or even not-so-good work—was often brutally frank."[9]

Over the years at various times, twenty-two different men attended the meetings of the Inklings. All were friends of C. S. Lewis, and all were drawn together by shared interests such as literature, religion, and general culture. Of this group, four stand out as being among the very closest friends Lewis had. These men influenced and enlightened him in spiritual matters, and they all were friends for their lifetimes.

Lewis first met J. R. R. Tolkien ("Tollers") in May 1926. He was twenty-eight; Tolkien was thirty-four. In *Surprised by Joy*, Lewis tells how that friendship with Tolkien helped him to break two of his old prejudices:

> I had been warned never to trust a Papist (Roman Catholic) . . . and never to trust a philologist (one who studies languages). Tolkien was both.[10]

When Lewis met Tolkien, he was at the point in his spiritual pilgrimage where he had to make a decision to either accept or reject God. In Tolkien he found not only an inspired storyteller and comparable scholar, but also a man of humor and charm and intellectual integrity who happened to be a devout Christian. The two men spent many hours together over several years talking about literature, history, and religion.

Lewis's essay on friendship in *The Four Loves* could be called a representation of much of his friendship with Tolkien. Their friendship began with the shared interests of story, especially Norse mythology or "northernness," and what is authentic in religion. Their friendship was never jealous and was shared by other friends; in fact they both "sought out the company of others." Both always enjoyed and sought out the "golden sessions" when they could be together and talk in complete freedom and acceptance of one another. After Lewis's conversion, both encouraged the other often, especially in the writing of their fantasy tales.

They had their problems, however, mainly on Tolkien's side. He was disappointed that Lewis never became a Catholic, and he never understood why Lewis would marry a divorced woman. Nevertheless, he always treated Lewis personally with courtesy and appreciation. His friendship with Jack was one of the great "compensations" of his life, and when Lewis died in 1963 (Tolkien lived another ten years), his friend wrote:

> We owed each a great debt to the other, and that tie with the deep affection . . . remains. He was a great man of whom the cold-blooded obituaries only scraped the surface.[11]

Shared interests drew Jack Lewis—Oxford professor, literary critic, and world-famous Christian apologist ("defender of the faith")—to Charles Williams, editor of the Oxford University Press, novelist, and poet. In 1936, when Lewis was thirty-seven, and Williams was forty-nine, the two men discovered each other's work and exchanged letters of appreciation. Lewis thanked Williams for his novel *The Place of the Lion*, and Williams thanked Lewis for his study of medieval tradition, *The Allegory of Love*. They agreed on many things, although the two were from radically different backgrounds.

Lewis was an Ulsterman from Belfast and had spent most of his adult life in Oxford. Williams had grown up in London, attended college for only two years, and worked most of his adult life in the publishing business. Lewis was still a bachelor, while Williams was married and had a small son. Lewis was a great lover of nature, and Williams loved cities. Lewis had a very charismatic personality and could be argumentative in literary debate. Williams was quieter and had a somewhat mystical quality about him. Yet their friendship flourished, and both influenced the other in profound ways.

Author Richard Sturch suggested that a common shared interest or theme that united these two very different men was "moralism," or a passionate interest in human goodness and love.[12] When Williams moved to Oxford from London in 1939, he and Lewis quickly became close and good friends and seemed to travel in the same spiritual world. Aside from literary interests—Plato, Dante, Blake, Milton, Wordsworth— they had theological interests in common. Both wrote about hell and purgatory in their works, the "double nature" of every person (a tendency toward both evil and good), and the idea of human romance as an agent of God's love.

The shared interest for which Lewis was most indebted to Williams was his idea of "substituted love," an idea that was later to become very personal for Lewis. Simply put, this means giving of oneself for others, or carrying another's burden. Lewis wrote about the concept of substituted love in his Narnia stories and *That Hideous Strength*; a person who gives unconditionally to others can come to a true realization of what humans were intended to be as creations of God.

Lewis's friend and fellow Inkling Nevil Coghill told how Jack believed he had the power, through Christian love, to accept in his body the pain of someone else. This was how God used him to ease the suffering of his wife Joy when she was dying. In talking to Coghill about his happy marriage, Lewis told him how he was to accept Joy's pain. "You mean," said Coghill, "that her pain left her, and that you felt it in your own body?" "Yes," Lewis said, "In my legs. It was crippling. But it relieved hers."[13] Lewis always thanked God for this gift of "substituted healing" for Joy. It provided for them both the time they needed to be together—at least for a while.

As with Tolkien, Lewis's friendship with Charles Williams is illustrated beautifully in *The Four Loves*. They shared common purposes and a Christian vision and a love for the deeper realms of spirituality. Lewis regarded Williams as a model for what Christian goodness really is and often tried to imagine what his friend would do in a time of personal doubt or temptation. After Williams died suddenly in 1945, Lewis wrote:

> No event has so corroborated my faith in the next world as Williams did simply by dying. When the idea of death and the idea of Williams thus met in my mind, it was the idea of death that was changed.[14]

Of all the people in the C. S. Lewis "canon," perhaps the least known is Major Warren H. "Warnie" Lewis. Jack's older brother was a career army officer and lifelong bachelor, and published seven books of seventeenth-century French history and biography. There is little public knowledge of Warnie Lewis's views on Christianity or of his personal reactions to his brother's early atheism, conversion, or fame as a Christian writer. Some information can be gained from *The Letters of C. S. Lewis* and the *Memoir* in that volume, as well as from his diary, *Brothers and Friends*. This diary is important for its rare records of some of the Inklings meetings and for details of Jack's friendship and marriage to Joy Gresham. Warnie always admired and accepted Joy, and by all accounts this friendship was mutual.

On the surface, Warnie and Jack seemed to have had very little in common. Jack was the academic man; Warnie was the military man, although he was widely read and shared many of his brother's likes and dislikes in books. Warnie had what could be called a "mild" personality; Jack could be "sharp" and cutting, especially in literary debate. Warnie was a "simple man," in the positive sense of the word; his brother was more complicated psychologically. Jack once wrote about his brother to a friend: "Dear Warnie, he's one of the simplest souls I know in a way, certainly one of the best at getting simple pleasures."[15] The two brothers were inseparable and lived together much of their lives, and both always regarded the other as his dearest and closest friend.

Warnie and Jack had one primary interest that enriched them on a spiritual level: love of simplicity in lifestyle and religion. Both brothers pursued the preservation of order in their everyday lives—"a sincere love of monotony," as Lewis described it. They both loved the solitude of long walks in the British countryside, and both intensely disliked the busyness and industrialization of their Oxford, which reached full flourish in the 1940s. The silence of a neighborhood early in the morning after a snowfall, the comfortable security of a fog, and a rainbow of flowers in an English garden were pleasures that increased in each other's company. Perhaps more often than anything else, the two brothers and friends were linked by shared memories of their boyhood in Ireland.

As to religion, neither Jack nor Warnie appreciated the music of hymns (probably because they were played and sung so poorly in their church) nor the "commotion" of the high (Anglican) church calendar, though both did enjoy the beauty of classical music and the quiet moments of "two or three gathered together." They loved the quiet serenity of churches and cathedrals, and when on their "walking tours" would always visit any small and pretty church they could find. A Christian event the two brothers shared is worth noting. When Jack received Communion for the first time as a convert, Warnie was stationed in Shanghai. By strange coincidence, Warnie received Communion on that same Christmas Day, 1931. It was not until much later that they both learned of the other's commitment.

Both Jack and Warnie were concerned about Warnie's chronic alcoholism. It is probably good that we do not have any record of conversations the two brothers had about this shared agony. Many times, in letters to other friends, Jack would mention his prayers and sometimes despair over Warnie's illness. He would ask others to pray for Warnie and often had friends "look out" for him when he could not. In *The Four Loves* Jack wrote these words that illustrate vividly what he believed friendship with a suffering brother meant:

> The mark of perfect friendship is not that help will be given when the pinch comes (of course it will) but that, having been given, it makes no difference at all . . . It was a distraction . . . a waste of the time, always too short, that we had together.[16]

## C. S. Lewis and His Friends: Women

In 1990, the British author A. N. Wilson published a major study about C. S. Lewis. This work was trumpeted as *the* biography on the *real* Lewis. Promotions for this book stated that its author had succeeded, like no previous biographer, in "bringing Lewis to life." In the book, Wilson mentioned that, among other things, Lewis was a rather unhappy, introspective, guilt-ridden figure who really disliked and feared women and who consummated his relationship with Joy Gresham *before* their Christian marriage at the Churchill Hospital.

Several of the promotional "blurbs" for the movie *Shadowlands* and the books that went with it implied the same thing, that Lewis "had no room for women in his perfectly ordered life," and that he was protected from women by his male friends and his busy literary career.

Of all the headlines in the life of Jack Lewis, there has been none so discussed as his "lack" of relationships with women and his late marriage to and "real" life with Joy Gresham. The truth is that he sustained many good friendships with women, and these were a great benefit to him spiritually.

Many scholars have said and written that Lewis was shy and "inexperienced" with women. This label is at least partially true, especially as it concerns his boyhood, adolescence, and young adult years. He had no sisters and only male friends as a child (his brother Warnie was prominent). His mother died when he was young. He disliked and was awkward at school sports. He spent much of his teenage years in all male schools and with a private tutor, plus attended and later taught at the predominantly male Oxford University.

Lewis did have several long and nurturing friendships with women as an adult, however, friendships that were significant factors in his spiritual growth and well-being. One good friend was Sister Penelope Lawson, the librarian at the St. Mary's Anglican convent at Wantage, about fifteen miles southwest of Oxford. She first wrote to Jack in 1939 after reading his book *Out of the Silent Planet*. Enclosed with her letter was a copy of her first book, *God Persists*, which had just been published; she later wrote and translated more than forty other books. This communication led to a close friendship that lasted until Jack's death.

In 1941, Sister Penelope invited Lewis to lecture to the junior nuns at St. Mary's, which he did in early 1942 and several times thereafter. He accepted the first invitation because he was a friend, but with some reluctance because of an old-fashioned Protestant aversion to religious life for women. He remarked to Penelope, "What very odd tasks God sets us! If anyone had told me ten years ago that I would be lecturing in a convent . . . !"[17] Jack found the young women there attentive and appreciative with intelligent questions. His first lecture was titled "The Gospel in Our Generation."[18] After Jack published *Perelandra* in 1947, he dedicated the book to "some ladies at Wantage." When the Portuguese edition came out, it was mistakenly translated "to some wanton ladies!"

Jack and Sister Penelope shared numerous things in their long friendship, including questions concerning spiritual matters, ideas about the books they were writing, literary insights, concerns over their own illnesses (both had bone diseases) and the afflictions of friends, many requests for prayer, and even thoughts about death. Just before his death, and after he went into a coma and nearly died a month or so earlier, Lewis wrote to Penelope,

> To be brought back and have all one's dying to do *again* was rather hard. If you die first, and if prison visiting is allowed, come back and look me up in purgatory.[19]

He thanked her many times for all that she had done for him and once added, "Who knows how much it may be?" Often he thanked her for the cheer and comfort she always gave him. In *The Four Loves* Lewis emphasizes that true friends are "traveling companions" on different journeys side by side. This description fits very well the friendship of Jack and Penelope, who were traveling companions for nearly twenty-five years. They shared a similar but also very different spiritual pilgrimage side by side, always praying and cheering and comforting one other. And I'm quite sure he eventually revised his opinion about "women in religious life."

Another woman who was good friends with Jack for many years was Ruth Pitter, who lived in the picturesque little village of Long Crendon, about twelve miles from Oxford. Ruth was considered one of England's finest poets and was the first woman to win the Queen's Gold Medal for poetry. Among her supporters were G. K. Chesterton's great friend Hilaire Belloc, Lewis's later friend David Cecil, and the novelist George Orwell.

Ruth heard Lewis on the radio in 1942, wrote to him, and was rescued from a severe depression by his talks and subsequent letters. Later, she became a Christian convert due primarily to his encouragement. After she and Lewis became friends, he visited her occasionally, both alone and with his brother Warnie. He was a great admirer of her poetry; she was one of the few "modern" poets he really enjoyed. When he sampled her poetry for the first time, he exclaimed, "Why didn't someone tell me [how wonderful a poet she is]?" He often would tell friends how delightful and witty and literary-minded Ruth was, and his letters to her fill an album an inch thick in Oxford's Bodleian Library.

Jack and Ruth were extremely "comfortable" friends; they obviously liked each other very much. He felt at ease and relaxed with her. They talked mostly about subjects domestic and literary. They both admired some of the same novelists and poets, and each humorously suggested nonsensical books for the other to write. The two also enjoyed gardening, and especially herb tasting. With Ruth, Jack always seemed peaceful and quiet and very happy.

Unknown to most persons, Jack considered marrying Ruth. George Sayer wrote that on one occasion in 1955, Lewis told him that if he were not a confirmed bachelor, Ruth Pitter would be the woman he would like to marry.[20] Most of the books and films about Lewis do not record that after his wife died, Jack went to see Ruth and confided in her. Several people alive today who knew Lewis and Ruth have stated that he might still have married her after Joy's death if he had been in better health.

The love Jack and Ruth had was perhaps a blending of the shared interests of friendship and the "warm comfortableness" of affection (*storge*). It satisfied both of them to be friends, and their friendship was not demanding or coercive. Both Ruth and Jack loved to be "homebodies," and both obviously enjoyed the "acceptance of domesticity" each gave the other. In *The Four Loves* Lewis wrote: "Affection at its best wishes neither to wound nor to humiliate nor to domineer."[21] Much to Ruth's regret, their friendship never grew into marriage, but she always accepted Jack as he was; and she always treated him with the common courtesy of Jesus Christ.

Of all of Jack's friends, none has been so criticized and misunderstood as Joy Davidman Gresham. Thanks to some excellent biographies and the recent films, we now know most of the particulars of her life and their life together. But even now, people resent her: some because she "invaded the life" of a confirmed bachelor and ended up marrying him, some because she was a Jew and a divorcée, some because they think he married her out of sympathy and because she "used" him, and some because she was not as "nice" as Ruth Pitter (whom many wish Lewis *had* married).

Interest in the friendship between Joy and Jack has been neglected, perhaps due to the emphasis on the romantic aspects of their story. We know that he was first attracted to her because she was tough-minded, witty, and had a realistic, non-sentimental approach to life. In *A Grief Observed*, Jack recalls that

> her mind was lithe and quick and muscular as a leopard . . .
> it scented the first whiff of cant or slush; then sprang, and
> knocked you over before you knew what was happening.
> How many bubbles of mine she pricked![22]

He was actually saying that Joy's friendship included the great gift of perceptive honesty—the ability to see persons as they really are and honestly accept them at the same time.

Admirers and romantics have questioned why Joy was not liked by some of Jack's friends. Perhaps the reason was jealousy, which Lewis mentioned often in *The Four Loves* as a prime deterrent to real friendship. Jack wrote that Joy was his "trusty comrade, friend, shipmate, fellow-soldier and mistress"; that she was "all any man friend has ever been to me"; and that if they had never fallen in love, they "would have nonetheless always been together and created a scandal." Based on these words, one can see how jealousy could find its way into the minds and hearts of many who cared about Jack.[23]

Jack Lewis loved many things, and loved them enthusiastically: books, nature, people, animals, domestic pleasures, beauty, authentic religion, good talk, good friends. In *A Grief Observed*, he mentions that Joy "liked more things and liked them more than anyone I have known."[24] We know that in their friendship Joy and Jack talked, prayed, argued, joked, assisted each other's literary projects, played Scrabble, worshiped, walked, traveled, despaired, hoped, and loved. We know also that as friends they pushed and pointed each other toward God and away from this world, or "the shadowlands."

Joy died on July 13, 1960, at the Radcliffe Infirmary in downtown Oxford. She was forty-five years-old. On the night she died, Austin Farrer and Lewis were in the room with her. At 11:20 P.M., she told Farrer, "I am at peace with God." Then Lewis saw her last smile, but it was not for him or Farrer. It was for someone else she saw in the room.[25] Both Joy and Jack were never the same again.

## C. S. Lewis as a Friend and Spiritual Mentor through Letters

In his letters we can learn much about Jack Lewis as one who took other persons' religious lives seriously, how he responded to their needs at the cost of his own time and energy, and how he was always ready to give some good reasons for "the hope that was in him." In many cases, his letters show him as a great friend who was also a spiritual director or mentor.

In Lewis's time, many people rarely or never used the telephone. They considered the weekly or even daily letter the expected way to communicate. In the beginning, Lewis's letters were to his father and brother; they maintained the ties of kinship and were written "in the line of duty." His late teens marked the beginnings of his letters to Arthur Greeves, a correspondence that lasted for the rest of Lewis's life. These letters are full of rich examples of affection, intelligence, and humor; but they are also valuable for the way they show us how Lewis changed from being an "arrogant prig" to a mature Christian.

Later, after he became world-famous as a literary critic and an apologist for the Christian faith, Lewis attracted a large variety of admirers who seemed heaven-bent on engaging him in personal and religious matters that he was expected to shed light on. From that time on, letter writing became a burden, an enormous demand on his time and his physical energies.

One may ask why Lewis continued writing letters. Maybe it was partly out of an Edwardian sense of obligation: One answered letters when they were sent; that was all there was to it! But more importantly, Lewis answered literally *all* the letters sent to him (with some help from his brother Warnie) because it was impossible for him to turn away from a genuine search for belief, a genuine cry for help. He considered answering letters a ministry, and he turned away no genuine request.

Lewis's responses to people became a form of spiritual mentoring, encouraging and guiding others as they faced questions of life and faith. Clyde Kilby wrote that the main reason Lewis answered letters so conscientiously was that he believed taking time out to advise or encourage another person was both a "humbling of one's talents before the Lord" and a way of allowing the Holy Spirit "to mold and mature a person"—himself.[26]

In his letters Lewis revealed a great deal of himself. He shared his own vulnerability and the difficulties of his faith; he was never afraid to tell someone about his own doubts and problems. In a letter to Arthur Greeves, he wrote:

> I think the trouble with me is lack of faith . . . the irrational deadweight of my old skeptical habits, and the spirit of this age, and the cares of the day, steal away all my lively feeling of the truth . . . when I pray I wonder if I am not posting letters to a non-existent address."[27]

And in a letter to a little girl ("Sarah") who had written him asking questions about Christianity, Lewis advised her not to worry about having certain "spiritual feelings" at her first Communion, and then added:

> For years after I had become a regular communicant, I can't tell you how dull my feelings were and how my attention wandered at the most important moments. It is only in the last year or two that things have begun to come right.[28]

These two letters were written about twenty years after his conversion. It is inspiring that no less a Christian of Lewis's stature wondered about his faith and prayers. When we read letters such as these, we can be assured that Jack was a person of character, one with whom we can identify.

The longest record of correspondence in which Lewis acted as a spiritual mentor is found in *Letters to an American Lady*. He never met Mary Shelbourne; her name was not revealed until after her death, hence "the American Lady" in the book title. She was a widow, a writer, and a woman who had many difficulties. She lost much of her money through unfortunate investments, had serious family and health problems (she nearly died twice), and had moved from the Episcopal tradition to Roman Catholicism. Thus, she had many questions about faith and doctrine.

Lewis wrote to Mary Shelbourne from 1950 until a few months before his death in 1963. Even though some of the letters are brief, his concern for this American lady is very evident. His letters reveal how spiritual mentoring or direction often goes past so-called religious subjects and God-talk. Lewis discussed everything with her from his gray "bullet-headed cat" to the books he was reading to where to find safety in a thunderstorm.

When Mary was faced with an unnamed "terrible affliction" (probably a serious illness), however, Lewis offered her sober advice and told her to live day by day and hour by hour and not worry about the future. Another time, he suggested that she not worry about other people's sins, but concentrate on her own. For the most part, the advice he gave her was presented in the framework of his own life. When she asked about distractions in prayer, he told her,

> What most interrupts my own prayers is not great distractions but tiny ones—things one will have to do or avoid in the course of the next hour.

Edward Sellner wrote that the common characteristic of Lewis's mentoring is "a willingness to share his own sacred journey in all its humanness, sorrows, and joy."[29] He told Mary of his marriage to Joy Gresham in 1956 and how "no one can mark the exact moment at which friendship becomes love." When his wife died four years later, he wrote of his loss and how he saw grief: "It isn't a state but a process."

Many of Lewis's letters to Mary show his delightful sense of humor. In 1958, he wrote to her about his and Joy's delayed honeymoon (at the Studley Priory Hotel near Oxford) and told her that he felt rather naughty "staying with a woman at a hotel! Just like people in the newspapers!" Another time, when Mary had evidently written to him about her anxieties about growing older, he wrote, "As for wrinkles—pshaw! Why shouldn't we have wrinkles? Honorable insignia of long service in this warfare."

The letters of C. S. Lewis show a man and a Christian who knew himself. He could confess without seeming to be self-indulgent or self-pitying. He could be clear about his own weaknesses such as arrogance or pride; but even in the most soul-searching of his letters, he maintained a counterbalance of the objective world and of the other person to whom he was writing. As is often the case in great letter writing, when one reads Lewis's letters, one is enhanced by all the aspects of his experiences . . . the lows as well as the highs.

## Notes

[1]James T. Como, ed., *C. S. Lewis at the Breakfast Table and Other Reminiscences* (New York: Macmillan, 1979) 192-201.

[2]Kathryn Lindskoog, *C. S. Lewis: Mere Christian* (Downers Grove IL: InterVarsity Press, 1981) 151.

[3]C. S. Lewis, *The Four Loves* (New York: Harcourt, Brace, Jovanovich, 1988) 62.

[4]For more on Lewis's views on the "inner ring," see the address by the same title in *The Weight of Glory*. In *That Hideous Strength*, the "hero," Mark Studdock, almost succumbs to the potential danger of the inner ring.

[5]C. S. Lewis, *The Four Loves*, 90.

[6]Ibid, 79.

[7]Clyde S. Kilby and Marjorie Lamp Mead, eds., *Brothers and Friends: The Diaries of Major Warren Hamilton Lewis* (San Francisco: Harper & Row, 1982) 182, n. 202.

[8]W. H. Lewis, quoted in George Sayer, *Jack: C. S. Lewis and His Times* (San Francisco: Harper & Row, 1988) 152.

[9]W. H. Lewis, *Letters of C. S. Lewis*, revised edition edited by Walter Hooper (Orlando FL: Harcourt Brace, 1993) 34.

[10]C. S. Lewis, quoted in Humphrey Carpenter, *Tolkien: A Biography* (Boston: Houghton Mifflin, 1977) 145.

[11]Humphrey Carpenter, ed., *The Letters of J. R. R. Tolkien* (Boston: Houghton Mifflin, 1981) 341.

[12]See Richard Sturch, "Common Themes Among Inklings," in *Charles Williams: A Celebration* (Leominster, Hertfordshire, England: Gracewing Fowler Wright Books, 1995) 153-75.

[13]John Lawlor, "The Tutor and Scholar," *Light on C. S. Lewis*, ed. Jocelyn Gibb (New York: Harcourt Brace, 1965) 63. See also Corbin S. Carnell, "The Friendship of C. S. Lewis and Charles Williams," *CSL: The Bulletin of the New York C. S. Lewis Society*, 7 (May 1985)16: 1-9.

[14]C. S. Lewis, ed., *Essays Presented to Charles Williams* (Grand Rapids MI: Eerdmans, 1974) xiv.

[15]Humphrey Carpenter, *The Inklings* (Boston: Houghton Mifflin, 1979) 38.

[16]C. S. Lewis, *The Four Loves*, 70.

[17]Carpenter, *The Inklings*, 184.

[18]The biography that contains the most information about Lewis and Sister Penelope, with many quotes from their letters, is William Griffin, *Clive Staples Lewis: A Dramatic Life* (Harper & Row, 1986).

[19]W. H. Lewis, *Letters*, 509.

[20]George Sayer, *Jack: A Life of C. S. Lewis* (Wheaton IL: Crossway Books, 2d ed., 1994) 344, 422. Kathryn Lindskoog reports that Lewis also said this to his friend and fellow Inkling Hugo Dyson. See *Light in the Shadowlands* (Sisters OR: Questar, 1994) 132.

[21]C. S. Lewis, *The Four Loves*, 44.

[22]C. S. Lewis, *A Grief Observed* (San Francisco: Harper & Row, 1989) 16-17.

[23]Ibid, 60.

[24]Ibid, 29.

[25]Lyle W. Dorsett, *And God Came In* (New York: Macmillan, 1983) 142.

[26]Clyde S. Kilby, ed., *C. S. Lewis: Letters to an American Lady* (Grand Rapids MI: Eerdmans, 1967) 7.

[27]Walter Hooper, ed., *They Stand Together: The Letters of C. S. Lewis to Arthur Greeves* (New York: Macmillan Press, 1979) 398-99.

[28]W. H. Lewis, *Letters*, 391.

[29]Edward C. Sellner, *Mentoring: The Ministry of Spiritual Kinship* (Notre Dame IN: Ave Maria Press, 1990) 46.

# Chapter 5

"But Look for Christ and You
Will Find Him, and with Him
Everything Else Thrown In"

L ife at the center helped produce in C. S. Lewis a particular type of lifestyle—one that matured over time, was open to change, and was uniquely Christian. His friend Luke Rigby described Jack this way:

> I know why he had friends. The kindness, sensitivity, the zest for life, the fun, the deep sense of humor, the seriousness, the depths, the unexpectedness: they combined to make a man who was exhilarating to be with.[1]

Lewis is one of the most reliable guides we have today for any seeker who wants a trustworthy model for authentic and reflective (but not dogmatic) Christian faith, and he certainly "practiced what he preached."

*Obedience* and *perseverance* are key words that were perhaps the foundation for Lewis's "life at the center." He learned early that obedience to God's wishes was to be primary for him, and that real change in a Christian's life only comes with much patience, hard work, and sacrifice. He also realized that the "basics" of prayer, devotion to the Bible, and God-centered friendships were what would "keep him keeping on" toward his goal of "becoming a little Christ"—which he said should be the goal of every Christian.

Jack's "life at the center" was disciplined and ordered. As a member of the Anglican church, he was a regular communicant and used *The Book of Common Prayer* at the church services he attended at Holy Trinity. During the school year, he would attend Dean's Prayers every morning at Magdalen College. And he would say his private prayers every morning before he left home, regardless of how he felt or where he was. If an emergency kept him from this, he would make time for his prayers in some other way.

Lewis kept what would be called today a "prayer list." He prayed not only for the conversion of people such as Sheldon and Jean Vanauken, but for friends such as his brother Warnie, Mary Shelbourne, Ruth Pitter, and Sister Penelope. He also prayed for the health and economic needs of his friends and for anyone else who wrote to him with requests.

Lewis meditated on the Scriptures when he prayed, especially when he was concerned about difficulties in his own life. Devotional Bible reading became a regular routine for him, and he read some portion of the Bible nearly every day. He remarked to a friend once that he did not mind being sick in bed with a cold or some "minor" ailment; this gave him more time to read the Bible and other books.

When one looks at the articles and sermons Lewis wrote, it is clear that he studied the Bible, and must have on regular and sustained basis. This is also borne out by the fact that he advised many persons who wrote to him about principles of biblical interpretation. In letters he gave counsel on how to solve "problem passages" in scripture, advice on biblical translations, and commentary on biblical persons and selected scriptures. He could not (and would not) have done this if he had not been totally immersed in the Bible, both in a devotional and contextual sense.

Lewis also used discipline and "arranged time" for his friendships. In addition to his bi-weekly meetings with the Inlings, he would take long yearly "walking tours" and shorter excursions with friends at fairly regular intervals, depending on his schedule and health. He would set aside Sundays and other times for answering letters—and he answered them all.

Despite the enormous demands on his time (especially after 1950), Lewis always made time for people who wanted to visit. Even a casual reading of the biographies will reveal that he spent much of his "free" time with friends and acquaintances over lunch, tea, or at pubs and hotels. He visited friends often, and one of the great pleasures of his life was to be able to spend extended periods of time with them, although these decreased in his later years due to health problems.

It is also noteworthy that Jack learned of the great value of spiritual guidance for himself. For years after he became a Christian, he would make routine visits to one of the Cowley Fathers (popularly known as the "Cowley Dads") at the Society of Saint John the Evangelist in Oxford, and there make confession and seek spiritual direction for his life. He did this until his director died many years later. We do not know how often Lewis prayed with his friends (except over meals), but he did pray with his taxi driver, Clifford Morris. Although this probably was not a regular habit, Lewis and

Morris did pray together after Joy's death. In fact, Morris may have been the first friend Lewis confided in.

Two areas that stand out in Lewis's life as having been significantly "changed for the better" due to his obedient and persevering "life at the center" are the recurring sin of pride and the difficulties of forgiveness. After his conversion, Lewis consciously set out to find the total implications of his faith. After intense self-examination, he found that his inner life and thinking were filled with ambition, pride, fears, hatreds, and lusts, among others. The worst problem was pride ("self-conceit"), which he wrestled with personally and wrote about for the rest of his life.

For many years, the change to Christianity was very difficult for Jack. In one letter to a friend he mentioned that the change he thought had occurred in his life "was only imaginary." But he slowly learned that his life as a Christian must start with the "death of ambition and pride." He wrote about the dangers of pride in *Mere Christianity*:

> For pride is spiritual cancer: it eats up the very possibility of love, or contentment, or even common sense . . . The real black, diabolical pride comes when you look down on others so much that you do not care what they think of you.[2]

Two stories illustrate just how far Lewis traveled in trying to overcome the sin of pride. In the summer of 1963, just before he died, a friend of his was talking to some of the dons at University College, where Lewis had been an undergraduate. When the friend told some of the men there that he knew Lewis, one of them shook his head and said something about Lewis being too proud. The friend reported later that the man's reaction surprised him as much as if he had said, "Mother Teresa is too selfish." The friend was flabbergasted, since he thought Jack to be the most humble person he had ever met. The next time he saw Jack, he told him about the incident and remarked how comical and absurd it all was. To his surprise, Lewis was hurt and then replied, "Oh, I was trying so hard to get over that! Apparently I haven't come as far as I had thought." When the friend apologized for telling him, Lewis insisted that he had done him an important service.[3]

The other story was told by Lewis's taxi driver, Clifford Morris. Lewis was a great preacher and communicator, and Morris always wondered why he was reluctant to preach more often than he did. One day Lewis had delivered a sermon and had received the usual kind words and congratulations from "all and sundry" present—which happened virtually every time he preached. In talking to Morris afterwards, he mentioned that he had begun to think "what a jolly fine and clever fellow Jack Lewis was," and then he added, "I had to get down on my knees pretty quickly to kill the deadly sin of pride!"[4]

Jack knew that pride was a perpetual nagging temptation, but he also knew there was help in overcoming it. In a letter to a Mrs. Sonia Graham, who had written him with questions about pride, he told her,

> We must keep on remembering that (grace) as a cure for pride . . . Keep on knocking it in the head, but don't be too worried about it. As long as one knows one is proud, one is safe from the worst form of pride.[5]

Thanks to his obedient and persevering prayers and help from friends, Jack received God's grace often in "knocking pride in the head."

After his conversion began, one thing Lewis did was to remember and reevaluate his personal relationships. In particular he tried very hard to forgive his father Albert, with whom he had an often very shaky and bitter relationship. When Albert died in 1929, it affected Jack profoundly. He felt ashamed of the way he had treated his father in the past, and he was determined to forgive Albert (and perhaps himself) and cleanse his life from the "weakness of character" that had caused him to act in such a way.

For about a week after Albert's death, Jack felt a strong sense of his father's presence. Lewis's friend George Sayer wrote that this "created or reinforced in him a belief in personal immortality and also influenced his conduct in times of temptation."[6] Jack forgave his father, and from then on, forgiveness was a Christian trait he tried very hard to develop fully and to maintain.

It took Lewis a very long time to realize what forgiveness really was and to believe in it with his whole being, and even then it was a gift of God's grace. In a letter to a friend, the Italian priest Don Giovanni Calabria, in 1951, he wrote:

> For a long time I believed that I believed in the forgiveness of sins. But suddenly this truth appeared in my mind in so clear a light that I perceived never before . . . had I believed it with my whole heart. So great is the difference between mere affirmation by the intellect and that faith . . . which the Apostle wrote was substance.[7]

When he was a boy, Jack had many traumatic and terrifying experiences at his early schools, which he describes in *Surprised by Joy*. At Wynyard, the headmaster was Robert Capron ("Oldie"), a clergyman in the Church of England. Capron was a "domestic tyrant" who would fly into rages and physically cane and mentally abuse the boys for the smallest offense. In at least once incident, Capron treated a boy with such brutality that the boy's father took him to court. The case was settled out of court, with the ruling against Capron. Wynyard closed shortly after Lewis left in 1910, and Capron was certified insane.

For more than fifty years, Jack Lewis felt anger and resentment toward Capron. Once he became a Christian, he tried hard to forgive Capron and to heal his almost obsessive resentment. On July 9, 1963, he was able to write these words to Mary Shelbourne concerning his struggle:

> Do you know, only a few weeks ago I realised suddenly that I at last had forgiven the cruel schoolmaster who so darkened my childhood. I'd been trying to do it for years . . . this time I feel it is the real thing . . . one is safe as long as one keeps on trying.[8]

Jack once wrote a little essay called "On Forgiveness." In it he mentions how difficult it is to learn to forgive the "incessant provocations of daily life" such as the bossy mother-in-law, the bullying husband, the nagging wife, and the deceitful son. He knew that these provocations can very easily become imbedded in one's life, and the longer one lives, the longer it takes to learn to forgive. The last words in that essay give hope and warning. These picture very well why forgiveness was so important to him and why he worked so hard at it. He asks the reader to remember Jesus' words in the model prayer about forgiving in order to receive forgiveness, and then adds,

> We are offered forgiveness on no other terms. To refuse it is to refuse God's mercy for ourselves. There is no hint of exceptions and God means what he says.[9]

## Notes

[1]See Luke Rigby, O. S. B., "A Solid Man," in *C. S. Lewis at the Breakfast Table and Other Reminiscences*, James Como, ed. (New York: Macmillan, 1979) 38-40.

[2]C. S. Lewis, *Mere Christianity* (London: Geoffrey Bles, 1952) 99-100. For Lewis's classic essay on pride, see "The Great Sin" in Chapter 8, Book III, *Christian Behaviour*.

[3]See Walter Hooper, "Remembering C. S. Lewis," *The Chesterton Review*, XVII, no. 3, XVII, no. 4 (August 1991 and November 1991): 369-71.

[4]Como, 200.

[5]W. H. Lewis, *Letters of C. S. Lewis*, revised edition edited by Walter Hooper (Orlando FL: Harcourt Brace, 1993) 422.

[6]George Sayer, *Jack: C. S. Lewis and His Times* (San Francisco: Harper & Row, 1988) 134.

[7]Martin Moynihan, ed., *Letters: C. S. Lewis—Don Giovanni Calabria* (Ann Arbor MI: Servant Books, 1988) 67.

[8]Clyde S. Kilby, ed., *C. S. Lewis: Letters to an American Lady* (Grand Rapids MI: Eerdmans, 1967) 117.

[9]C. S. *Lewis, Fern-Seed and Elephants and Other Essays on Christianity* (Glasgow, Scotland: Collins/Fount, 1986) 43.

# Conclusion
# and
# Reflection

In September 1992, I took a long anticipated trip to Lewis's Oxford and Cambridge. I had been reading and studying about this man for over twenty years. This trip was one of the very high points of my entire life. Aside from the picture taking and souvenir buying and book hunting and old church gazing, I wanted to do something else. I wanted to somehow experience the life and times and places of C. S. Lewis in a spiritual sense, something I could not put into words. I wanted to walk where he had walked. I wanted to worship where he had worshiped. I wanted to eat and drink where he had eaten and drank. I wanted to study where he had studied. And I did.

I walked many times along the High, one of the most famous streets in the world. Lewis must have taken the same walk hundreds of times. I traveled along Addison's Walk, the beautiful 800-year-old path that makes a semicircle around the deer park just behind where Lewis taught for thirty years at Magdalen College. It was on this walk that he became convinced of the truth of the Christian story 'way back in the 1930s. While at Magdalen College, I walked around the cloisters where some of *Shadowlands* was filmed, visited the famous chapel there where he worshiped often, and looked up at those celebrated rooms in New Buildings where he met students for thirty years and hosted Inklings meetings.

And speaking of the Inklings, I was fortunate to make several trips to the "Bird and Baby" pub, where Lewis and his famous friends had so many hours of wonderful talk and laughter. I saw the pictures of Tolkien and Williams and Warren and Joy and all the rest, and I sat right next to the fireplace where Jack always dumped his pipe ashes.

I worshiped in St. Mary's church and looked up at the 500-year-old pulpit where Lewis preached "The Weight of Glory" and where John Wesley, Cardinal Newman, and William Temple had preached so many times. I went from St. Mary's up the High, turned right on Longwall, and entered the Cross Church medieval cemetery where many of Lewis's friends, students, and influences are buried: the writer and poet Charles Williams, his best friend; the Inkling Hugo Dyson, who, with Tolkien, helped lead Jack to faith; the great Anglican theologian Austin Farrer, who presided over the funerals of both Jack and Joy; Kenneth Tynan, his most brilliant student; James Blish, the great science fiction writer who dedicated a book to Lewis; Kenneth Grahame, whose *Wind in the Willows* Lewis read and reread his entire life.

I visited Lewis's home church (Holy Trinity) in Headington and was allowed to meditate there alone for about thirty minutes or so. An old gentleman working there gave me a *Book of Common Prayer* from the church; he jokingly told me that "C. S. Lewis himself" might have used it. I stood beside Jack and Warren's grave in that same churchyard, and I must have read the Shakespeare inscription on their stone a hundred times: "Men must endure their going hence."

I went where Jack and Warnie and Mrs. Moore and Fred Paxford the gardener and assorted dogs, cats, and birds had lived. I saw Joy's garden, then sadly overrun with weeds. The Kilns is about a hundred yards down "Lewis Close," which is right off "Kiln Lane." I went inside the old house and looked at Jack's ancient loveseat and his faded, battered, old light maroon sofa—which had a piece of masking tape across it so as to discourage visitors from sitting on it. I saw his library, where he had written so many words that have moved me and countless others. I saw where he had eaten and slept and paced and prayed.

Later on, back in the "city centre," I passed his barbershop—where he hated to go because he hated getting haircuts. I spent as much time as I could at the great Bodleian Library, where he practically lived for years. I visited his other pubs: "The Lamb and Flag," "The King's Arms," "The Trout." I lurked around his bookshops: Blackwells, Thorntons, Waterfields. I saw Ronald Tolkien's house and Lewis's favorite tree in the Botanic Garden, where the last picture of him was taken. I went to the Fellow's Garden at Wadham College and saw the oldest tree in Oxford, a place where Lewis and his friend and lawyer Owen Barfield must have had many of the philosophical and religious discussions they later called "The Great War." I saw all of these, and a whole lot more.

As I mentioned, I had traveled to Oxford to experience C. S. Lewis and his cities and his times. After years of study and giving so many "C. S. Lewis seminars" to churches, I wanted to have some kind of spiritual "happening" at Oxford. I thought if I retraced some of the steps of the most spiritual person I've ever read about, I would have an encounter with God, or become more spiritual, or learn more about spirituality, or "grow" spiritually, or something.

In retrospect, I know now that I was a very poor student of C. S. Lewis (and probably of the Scriptures). Lewis's "life at the center" was a gift from God, a gift of grace. God gave Jack the vehicles of prayer, the Bible, and good friendships to help him become a little more like God's son, who is the Christ. Lewis came to know that this takes time, constant obedience, and perseverance; for him, it took a whole lifetime. He also knew that "being spiritual" is not a "happening" or an "event." He knew from long experience that he could never be so presumptuous as to try to "plan" spirituality.

Why is C. S. Lewis such a good model for the Christian today? A clue might be found in his last words from *Mere Christianity*. In his explanation of how the Christian life ought to be on the practical level of daily living, Lewis wrote: "But look for Christ and you will find Him, and with Him everything else thrown in." Here is a man who found Christ, and the world has been a better place ever since. And the Christ in Jack Lewis can teach us so many things. He can teach us that consistency and hard work and attitude in prayer is vital, as is the necessity of praying always for other people.

He can teach us to look at the whole message, "the big picture," of the Bible and not get bogged down in the little messages of denominational squabbles. He can teach us to seek out and cherish Christian friends of like mind and heart and make time to be with them. He can teach us about remembrance and hope as we take the Communion bread and wine. And he can teach us to do all of this with good humor and a relaxed, reverential attitude toward the life that God has given each of us.

A friend of his once said that Jack Lewis was a man who "wished with all his heart to honor God's truth in every idea passing through his mind." The good news for Christians today is that if they will listen and be teachable, at least part

of God's truth can become real to them, as it was modeled by
C. S. Lewis. I hope I remember that when I take my next trip
to Oxford.

# Appendixes

# Appendix A

## Chronology
## The Life and Influence of C. S. Lewis

CHILDHOOD

1898    Born in Belfast, Ireland, to Albert and Flora Lewis

1902    Chose the name Jack ("Jacksie") for life

1905    Family moved to "Little Lea" in Country Down, suburb of Belfast

1908    Read Milton's *Paradise Lost*; mother died of cancer; Jack and brother Warren sent to Wynyard school in England

ACADEMIC PURSUITS

1909    Suffered at poorly-run boarding school

1911    Entered Cherbourg School; lost childhood faith

1912    Discovered Wagner and Norse mythology

1913    Won scholarship at Malvern College

1914    Met lifelong friend Arthur Greeves and first influential teacher, Arthur T. Kirkpatrick ("The Great Knock")

1915    Discovered writings of George MacDonald (*Phantastes*), the man who "baptized his imagination"

1916    Accepted at Oxford's University College

1917    Began studies at University College; entered the army and met the Moore family

1918    Wounded in France and returned to England

1919    Published first book of poetry, *Spirits in Bondage*, under pseudonym "Clive Hamilton"

1920    Achieved academic success: a first in "Honor Mods" (philosophy)

1922    Achieved academic success: a first in "Greats" (classics)

1923    Achieved academic success: a first in English (literature)

1925    Gained permanent position as tutor at Magdalen College, Oxford

1926    Published second book of poetry, *Dymer*; met J. R. R. Tolkien

1928    Began writing his first great scholarly work, *The Allegory of Love*

1929    Father Albert died in September; Lewis regained belief in God

1930    Moved into permanent home, "The Kilns"

INCREASING ACCOMPLISHMENTS

1931    Accepted Christianity
1933    Wrote first Christian book, *The Pilgrim's Regress*
1936    Discovered Charles Williams's *The Place of the Lion*
1938    Published first science fiction work, *Out of the Silent Planet*
1939    Preached the sermon "Learning in War-Time"; published
        *Rehabilitations* and *The Personal Heresy*
1940    Published *The Problem of Pain*; conceived the idea for *The
        Screwtape Letters* in church
1941    Began series of twenty-five wartime radio broadcasts;
        preached most famous sermon, "The Weight of Glory"
1942    Published *The Screwtape Letters*, *A Preface to Paradise
        Lost*, and *Broadcast Talks*; preached famous sermon,
        "Miracles"
1943    Published *The Abolition of Man*, *Perelandra* (second of
        "space trilogy"), and *Christian Behaviour*
1944    Published *Beyond Personality*; delivered the oration "The
        Inner Ring" in London
1945    Close friend Charles Williams died; published the essay,
        "Work and Prayer," and *That Hideous Strength* (third of
        "space trilogy")
1946    Awarded honorary Doctor of Divinity, St. Andrews
        University
1947    Published *Miracles*; appeared on the cover of *Time* maga-
        zine
1948    Recorded preface to *The Great Divorce* for BBC Radio; pub-
        lished *Arthurian Torso*
1949    Published *Transposition and Other Addresses*, later *The
        Weight of Glory*; the first critical study was written about
        Lewis, Chad Walsh's *C. S. Lewis: Apostle to the Skeptics*
1950    Published *The Lion, the Witch, and the Wardrobe*; received
        first letter from Joy Davidman
1951    Published *Prince Caspian*; "surrogate mother" Mrs. Moore
        died; declined Churchill's offer of Commander of the British
        Empire
1952    Awarded honorary Doctor of Literature, Laval University,
        Quebec; published *The Voyage of the "Dawn Treader"*
1953    Published *The Silver Chair;* read Arthur C. Clarke's
        *Childhood's End*
1954    Appointed Professor of Medieval and Renaissance Literature
        at Cambridge; published monumental work, *English
        Literature in the Sixteenth Century*; published *The Horse
        and His Boy*; taught last tutorial at Oxford

1955   Published *The Magician's Nephew* and *Surprised by Joy*
1956   Published *The Last Battle* and *Til We Have Faces*; married Joy Davidman in civil ceremony at Oxford registry office
1957   Married Joy Davidman while she was in the hospital dying of cancer; awarded honorary Doctor of Letters, University of Manchester
1958   Published *Reflections on the Psalms*
1959   Wife Joy suffered relapse; wrote *Screwtape Proposes a Toast*
1960   Joy died after trip to Greece; published *The Four Loves*, *Studies in Words*, and *The World's Last Night*
1961   Published *A Grief Observed* under pseudonym, "N. W. Clerk," and *An Experiment in Criticism*
1962   Began writing *Letters to Malcolm: Chiefly on Prayer* and published *They Asked for a Paper*
1963   Wrote last article (for *The Saturday Evening Post*); died November 22, the same day as John F. Kennedy and Aldous Huxley; friend Roger L. Green published first book study on Lewis as a children's writer

AFTER DEATH

1964   *Poems*, *Letters to Malcolm*, and *The Discarded Image* published; *The Christian World of C. S. Lewis* published by Clyde Kilby
1965   Major critical study, *Light on C. S. Lewis*, published; Marion E. Wade Center at Wheaton College established
1966   *Studies in Medieval and Renaissance Literature* and *Of Other Worlds* published
1967   *Letters of C. S. Lewis* published by Warren Lewis; also *Christian Reflections*, *Letters to an American Lady*, and *Spenser's Images of Life*; first book about Lewis written by a Baptist published, Richard Cunningham's *C. S. Lewis: Defender of the Faith*
1969   New York C. S. Lewis Society established; *Narrative Poems and Selected Literary Essays* published
1970   *God in the Dock* published
1973   Major Warren Lewis and J. R. R. Tolkien died in Oxford; Kathryn Lindskoog published *C. S. Lewis: Mere Christian*
1974   First biography about Lewis written by Walter Hooper and Roger L. Green
1975   *Fern-Seed and Elephants* published
1977   *The Dark Tower* and Sheldon Vanauken's *A Severe Mercy* published

1979    *They Stand Together: C. S. Lewis's Letters to Arthur Greeves* published
1982    *C. S. Lewis on Stories* and *Of This and Other Worlds* published
1983    First biography of Joy Davidman, *And God Came In*, published by Lyle Dorsett
1985    *Letters to Children* and *Boxen* published
1986    *Present Concerns* published
1988    *Letters: C. S. Lewis—Don Giovanni Calabria* published; biography, *Jack: C. S. Lewis and His Times*, published by friend George Sayer
1991    Early diary *All My Road Before Me* published
1994    Kathryn Lindskoog published *Light in the Shadowland— Protecting the Real C. S. Lewis*; Peter Kreeft published *C. S. Lewis for the Third Millennium*
1995    John A Sims's *Missionaries to the Skeptics* published, first book about Lewis published by a Baptist Press (Mercer University Press)

# Appendix B

## C. S. Lewis and Communion

On both of my study trips to Lewis's Oxford, I visited his home church, Holy Trinity, in the suburb of Headington. During the last visit, I met a retired elder of the church who doubled as caretaker and sexton. He graciously invited me in, gave me a "tour" and short history of the old church, and very warmly answered my many questions about Lewis and his brother Warren—questions he no doubt had been asked many times by the hundreds of Lewis "fans" who visit Oxford yearly.

When I asked him about Lewis's worship habits, he told me that "everyone knows that Lewis came to church mainly for the sacrament of Communion." He further added that Lewis sometimes would have Communion administered to him at home (The Kilns, about a mile away) if he was ill, and if the rector or another minister from Holy Trinity was available. The elder also mentioned that Lewis and his wife Joy often shared Communion at home in 1959–1960, when she was very ill.

C. S. Lewis received Communion at Holy Trinity church for the first time on Christmas day, 1931. This was a short time after his conversion to Christianity, a gradual process from 1926 to 1931; he had not taken Communion since his boyhood days in Belfast. In his first years as a Christian, he took the sacrament only on Christmas and Easter, then later once a month. During the last fifteen or so years of his life, he normally received Communion every week.

The practice of receiving Communion was obviously very important to Lewis, and it was an important part of his overall spiritual outlook. For him, the taking of the cup and the wine symbolized obedience to Christ and a participation in the mystery of God as revealed in Christ. One explanation for his love of this sacrament was its private nature, and his own tendency toward shyness around people he did not know very well. He especially enjoyed the private communions he shared with Joy and his priest; in fact, he probably preferred them to those in church. "Church" was often a distraction to Lewis. He did not like church music particularly, especially hymns played or sung badly, and "church business matters" irked him as well.

The elder at Holy Trinity told me that after Jack and Warren received Communion, they would leave the church, often before the "service" was over; an usher would hold the door open for them as they left not so quietly, with Jack's walking stick tapping the floor.

When I asked him if he thought Lewis was being aloof or not willing to be friendly, he answered that the reason was because of Lewis's incredibly busy schedule. Sunday was usually the only day he could catch up on his voluminous correspondence (especially in the later years when he became world famous) and spend quality time with his brother.

Lewis was a member of the Anglican Church, and as such was a faithful consultant of *The Book of Common Prayer*. Its "Articles of Religion" state that when a person partakes of the Communion elements with integrity—for Lewis this meant realistic hope and confessional honesty—that person identifies with Christ and will receive nourishment for the soul.

When surveying letters and anecdotes from Lewis's friends about his understanding of Communion, it is difficult to gain a consensus as to how much he actually understood about what Communion actually *does* for a person. One common element in his friends' comments, however, is that Lewis had a strong sense for the need to obey the commands of Christ and to take the Communion in faith. It is also evident that the longer Lewis partook of Communion on a regular basis, the more he enjoyed it and looked forward to it. And I believe that this enjoyment came not just from the satisfaction of knowing that he was being obedient to Christ. C. S. Lewis's soul was nourished and cleansed and refreshed, at least in part, from his partaking of Communion in faith and with integrity. We have his life as proof.

## Appendix C

## Prayer
## Works by C. S. Lewis

Letter Four of *The Screwtape Letters* (1942) is considered by
many to be a classic essay about prayer. It is a warning from
Screwtape to Wormwood about "the painful subject" of prayer, its
nature and purpose plus distractions in prayer. In Letter Twenty-
Seven, Lewis has Screwtape order Wormwood to try to make the
young couple gain a "false spirituality" by noting that all petitionary
prayers are not answered right away and that some answered
prayers are really just the laws of nature working.

"On Special Providences," in *Miracles* (1947), is an essay deal-
ing with the providence of God and how prayer does or does not
influence providence.

*The Chronicles of Narnia* (seven volumes, 1950–1956) contain
several references to prayer, both explicit and implicit. In *The
Voyage of the "Dawn Treader,"* Lucy's prayer for deliverance from
the darkness "in the land where nightmares come true" is answered
in Aslan's coming in the form of an albatross to lead the ship to safe,
sunlit sea. In *The Silver Chair*, Eustace Clarence Scrubb and Jill
Pole call for Aslan with simple and obedient words, two of Lewis's
requirements for authentic prayer. And in *The Magician's Nephew*,
Digory's prayers for his mother to be healed with a piece of magic
fruit are answered by Aslan, but only after Digory is confronted with
his previous arrogance after a long and difficult journey.

"The Efficacy of Prayer" in *The World's Last Night and Other
Essays* (1960) was first printed in the *Atlantic Monthly* in 1959. In
this famous essay, Lewis answers questions about prayer and how it
works. It has been reprinted many times.

*Letters to Malcolm: Chiefly On Prayer* (1963) was the first book
by Lewis published after his death. Similar in style to *The Screwtape Letters*, it is a series of fictitious letters to a friend asking
questions and "comparing notes" about prayer.

*Poems* (1964) contains several short selections that deal with
prayer. These are "Prayer"; "The Apologist's Evening Prayer;"
"Footnote to All Prayers," originally in *The Pilgrim's Regress*, 1933;
and "After Prayers, Lie Cold." The latter was probably written after
and in response to Joy Lewis's death.

"Petitionary Prayer: A Problem Without an Answer" in *Christian Reflections* (1967) is an address Lewis gave to a group of
Oxford ministers in 1953.

All of Lewis's collections of letters contain many references to petitionary prayer and his own personal prayer life. There are currently six collections of Lewis's letters in print: *The Letters of C. S. Lewis* (1915–1963), *Letters to an American Lady* (103 letters from 1950–1963), *They Stand Together* (written to his friend Arthur Greeves, 1914–1963), *Letters to Children* (1944–1963), and the *"Latin" Letters of C. S. Lewis to Don Giovanni Calabria* (1947–1961). Sheldon Vanauken's classic, *A Severe Mercy* (1977), contains eighteen short letters by Lewis that mention his prayerful concern for the salvation of two young American students in Oxford.

*God in the Dock* (1970) contains two essays with significant sections on prayer: "Work and Prayer" (a newspaper article published in 1945) and "Scraps" (first printed in 1945 in a church journal). The former is Lewis's answer to a common "problem" of prayer: If God is all wise and all good, why do we have to pray?

## Appendix D

## The Bible
## Works by C. S. Lewis

Much of Lewis's book *Miracles* (1947) is devoted to a straightforward defense of the biblical accounts of the miraculous, including the "grand miracle" of the Incarnation. *The Voyage of the "Dawn Treader,"* third of the Narnia tales, tells of a journey full of miracles, ending with a telling of "the Greatest Miracle" in which the Christ-figure Aslan appears to the children with a message of salvation and hope. "Miracles" and "The Grand Miracle," both originally sermons, appear in *God in the Dock.*

In *Transposition and Other Addresses* (1949, in *America: The Weight of Glory and Other Addresses*) Lewis published three sermons that have significant sections about the Bible. The text for "Learning in War-Time," a sermon he preached in autumn 1939, was Deuteronomy 26:5. In Oxford in June 1941, he preached his most famous sermon, "The Weight of Glory," based on 2 Corinthians 4:16-18 and focusing on heaven. He preached "Transposition" at Mansfield College Chapel, Oxford, May 1944. The textual basis was from the opening chapters of the book of Acts, and the sermon centered around the coming of the Holy Spirit to the early church.

Lewis wrote an introduction to J. B. Phillips's translation of the New Testament epistles, called *Letters to Young Churches* (1957). In it he discusses the need for new translations of the Bible and why Christians should read Paul's letters. This essay was later titled "Modern Translations of the Bible" in *God in the Dock.*

*Reflections on the Psalms* (1958) is Lewis's only book about the Bible. In it he describes the pleasures he gained from the psalter. The chapter titled "Scripture" centralizes Lewis's views about the Bible and how Christians are to approach it.

*Christian Reflections* (1967) contains two biblically related essays. "The Psalms" was written around the same time as *Reflections on the Psalms* and is more or less a summation of the book. "Modern Theology and Biblical Criticism" was originally an oral address read at Cambridge in 1959, and was Lewis's answer to the "modern theology" of his day that attempted to de-emphasize the miraculous elements of the Bible.

His essay "The Literary Impact of the Authorised Version" was originally a lecture at the University of London in 1950. It first appeared in book form in *They Asked for a Paper* (1962), and has been reprinted numerous times.

Michael J. Christensen, *C. S. Lewis on Scripture* (1979), contains a letter from Lewis to the American scholar Corbin Carnell (4 April 1953) and notes from a letter by Lewis to Clyde S. Kilby of Wheaton College. In the former Lewis discusses his view of the historicity of the Bible, and in the latter he lists specific biblical passages that pose problems in determining historicity.

There are many references to the Bible, biblical themes, biblical persons, biblical events, and specific biblical passages in Lewis's *Mere Christianity*, *The Problem of Pain*, *The Great Divorce*, *The Four Loves*, and his collections of letters.

# Appendix E

## "Life at the Center"
## Works about C. S. Lewis

The best biography of C. S. Lewis is *Jack* (revised 1994, paperback), written by his former student and close friend George Sayer. The first biography of Lewis was written by Roger Lancelyn Green and Walter Hooper (1974, available in paperback). Other biographies include those by William Griffin (1986), A. N. Wilson (1990), and Michael Coren (1994).

Humphrey Carpenter, *The Inklings* (1979), is the only book-length study of Lewis and his friends. Carpenter, *Tolkien* (1974), has a valuable chapter titled "Jack," which gives insights into the friendship of Lewis and Tolkien. Alice M. Hadfield, *Charles Williams: An Exploration of His Life and Work* (1983), contains many anecdotes and details of Lewis's friendship with Williams, as does the *Preface of Lewis's Essays Presented to Charles Williams*. Gareth Knight, *The Magical World of the Inklings* (1990), has a helpful overview of the Inklings as a group, plus individual chapters on Lewis, Williams, Tolkien, and Owen Barfield. *Owen Barfield on C. S. Lewis*, ed. G. B. Tennyson (1989), gives many personal insights into the friendship between Barfield and Lewis based on interviews, essays, and poems. *The Golden String* (1954), the autobiography by Lewis's good friend and former student, Dom Bede Griffith, includes many warm references to Lewis and their friendship. Sheldon Vanauken, *A Severe Mercy* (1977, available in paperback), is the longest single account of Lewis's influence on and friendship with specific persons. Vanauken and his wife Jean ("Davy") were students at Oxford in the 1950s and were converted largely due to the friendship and encouragement of Lewis.

C. S. Lewis, *The Four Loves* (1960), and its second chapter, "Friendship," is a deserved classic. Word Audio Books (Dallas TX) has recently issued *The Four Loves* on two cassettes, the only available recording of Lewis's own voice. The tapes serve as the basis for the book and are different in content. An excellent supplemental work is Isabel Anders, *The Faces of Friendship* (Cowley, 1992).

The three major biographies about Joy Davidman Gresham and her life, marriage, and friendship with C. S. Lewis are: Lyle W. Dorsett, *And God Came In* (1983, available in paperback); Brian Sibley, *C. S. Lewis Through the Shadowlands* (1985, available in paperback); and Douglas H. Gresham, *Lenten Lands* (1988, available in paperback). All contain helpful insights, especially Dorsett.

James Como, *C. S. Lewis at the Breakfast Table and Other Reminiscences* (1979, available in paperback), is a very valuable collection of twenty-four essays about Lewis written by friends, former students, colleagues, and admirers.

The diary of his brother Warren ("Warnie") H. Lewis, *Brothers and Friends* (1982, ed. Clyde S. Kilby & Marjorie L. Mead), contains many "intimate portraits" of C. S. Lewis the person and best friend. Warren's *Memoir in Letters of C. S. Lewis* (revised edition 1988, available in paperback) is the best short introduction to his brother's life and gives several anecdotes of Jack as friend and spiritual mentor.

Michael J. Christensen, *C. S. Lewis on Scripture* (1979, available in paperback), is the only book-length treatment of C. S. Lewis and the Bible. This work synthesizes Lewis's thoughts on the nature of biblical inspiration and revelation and how his ideas on the Bible relate to the "inerrancy" controversy. Mark E. Freshwater, *C. S. Lewis and the Truth of Myth* (1988), has a helpful section on Lewis's views on themes from the New Testament: Jesus, the Kingdom of God, the miraculous, and the historical validity of the Gospels.

Of works that discuss Lewis and prayer, the three best are: Kathryn Lindskoog, *C. S. Lewis: Mere Christian* (1973); Perry LeFevre, *Understandings of Prayer* (1981); and Richard Harries, *C. S. Lewis: The Man and His God* (1987). Lindskoog's treatment is especially valuable for her uniting of Lewis's "theory" of prayer with his "practical life" of prayer.

Of the many works that specifically discuss Lewis's *Letters to Malcolm* and *Reflections on the Psalms*, the best ones for the general reader are Clyde S. Kilby, *The Christian World of C. S. Lewis* (1964, available in paperback); Chad Walsh, *The Literary Legacy of C. S. Lewis* (1979, available in paperback, the "sequel" to his *C. S. Lewis: Apostle to the Skeptics*, 1949, the first book written about Lewis); Margaret P. Hannay, *C. S. Lewis* (1981); and Joe R. Christopher, *C. S. Lewis* (1987, in the Twayne's English Authors series).

Edward C. Sellner, *Mentoring: The Ministry of Spiritual Kinship* (Notre Dame IN: Ave Maria Press, 1990), has a perceptive and well-written chapter on C. S. Lewis as spiritual mentor and friend through his tutoring, preaching, and letter writing.

Of the journal articles published about Lewis's spirituality, many are available for the general reader. The *Chesterton Review* (St. Thomas More College, 1437 College Drive, Saskatoon, SK, Canada S7N OW6) published a special "C. S. Lewis Issue" in 1991 that contains nine memoirs by Lewis's friends. Nancy-Lou Patterson published an excellent essay, "The Spirituality of C. S. Lewis," in *The Canadian C. S. Lewis Journal*, Spring 1995 (U. S. address Box 70, Sumas, WA 98295). *CSL: the Bulletin of the New York C. S. Lewis Society* (the oldest Lewis society, established in the late 1960s) has published many articles about Lewis's friendships, influences, books, and spirituality. A listing can be obtained from Clara Sarrocco (84-23 77th Avenue, Glendale, NY 11385). Other C. S. Lewis journals of note are *VII: An Anglo-American Literary Review* (Wheaton College), and *The Lamp-Post of the Southern California C. S. Lewis Society.*